Seventy Thousand Veils

The Miracle of Energy

Seventy Thousand Veils

The Miracle of Energy

Claire Porter

BOOKS

Winchester, UK
Washington, USA

First published by O-Books, 2010
O-Books is an imprint of John Hunt Publishing Ltd., Laurel House, Station Approach,
Alresford, Hants, SO24 9JH, UK
office1@o-books.net
www.o-books.com

For distributor details and how to order please visit the 'Ordering' section on our website.

ISBN: 978 1 84694 395 9

A CIP catalogue record for this book is available from the British Library.

Design: Stuart Davies

Printed in the UK by CPI Antony Rowe
Printed in the USA by Offset Paperback Mfrs, Inc

CONTENTS

"God is the Light of the Heavens and the Earth."
The Koran

PROLOGUE

NO MAN IS AN ISLAND

'No man is an island, entire of itself."
John Donne (1572? – 1631)

As a child I often saw and heard 'dead people'.

I also travelled astrally at night – though I had no idea at the time that this was what I was actually doing. I called it 'flying' and I loved it. But, when I told my mother one evening that the 'little girl' at the back door felt cold and wanted to 'go to Heaven', she told me very firmly to be quiet, say my prayers and climb back into bed!

I continued to 'see' and 'play' with the same sad child for another three years, until one afternoon my younger sister boldly announced to my mother that she, too, could see 'Biddy', as we called her. With four children to look after and another baby on the way, this was all a bit too much for my poor mother. She put our coats on and then marched us up to the local Dominican Priory and demanded to speak with one of the Friars. As a devout Irish Catholic, my mother had been brought up to believe in an afterlife and this matter was, in her opinion, definitely a job for the Church! Shortly afterwards, a young Priest came to the house, interviewed my sister and myself and then began a special ritual that I now know to be a form of spirit releasement.

We never saw 'Biddy' again.

As I grew up and left my childhood years behind, I began to grow increasingly ashamed of this strange 'gift' that allowed me to see the dead, to sense 'bad people', to 'read' others' innermost feelings and sometimes even to see terrible things. It was my 'secret' and one that I definitely wanted to keep hidden. So I started on the long road to denial and set my sights firmly on the physical world. This was London in the 1980s and it was an extraordinary place to be – the punk rock era had begun, angry young men and dark haired girls dressed in black plastic bin liners held together with large safety pins, roamed the streets; the music was raw, emotional and confronting. We had a woman Prime Minister at No.10, were in the grip of the worst economic recession since the Second World War and the European Union was starting to spread its tentacles across the English Channel.

I became a journalist and for the next twenty years as a member of the media, I travelled the world and was privileged to see and meet many unusual and exceptional people from all strata of society. But this strange gift never left me.

There is an old Buddhist saying: "when the student is ready, the Teacher arrives". I finally learnt to channel this energy via dowsing. Dowsing is a means of 'reading' spiritual energy both within the earth and all sentient beings. I began to accept and to respect this gift for I was at last able to help others. But this was when the 'trouble', as I called it, started: for my 'awakening' was also to be a baptism of fire – an immersion in the pure white energy of God, from whom all psychics on the right hand path draw their strength - and a fierce battle with demonic fire from those on the left hand path who also entered my life at this time.

The first hard lesson I learnt was that positive energy attracts dark energy. And although the case itself is far too long to recount here, in essence I became the target of a very pronounced and deliberate psychic attack of the darkest possible kind. It left me a physical wreck for nearly four years until 'help' arrived in the form of a 94 year-old dowser called George who became my teacher and my guide. So strong was George's personal energy field that within minutes of sitting next to him the debilitating migraine that had plagued me for such a long time, simply evaporated. I began to feel well again, at peace and 'energized'. It was as if my psychic 'batteries' had been recharged, which, of course, they had!

With great compassion, George helped me to understand many things about the spiritual domain. Once fear and anger left me, I was back in control and I was able to take charge of the situation and deal with it relatively easily and safely. Other people, whose names I will not mention, also played key roles in clearing this deep demonic energy at other specific levels. Suffice to say, the situation was resolved, and the dark energy released. It has never returned to bother either my family or myself again.

Having spent some years engaged in 'energy work', as I call it, I decided that it was time to write this book.

This is not another motivational, warm and cozy 'read' on the spiritual world and it contains information and case studies across the energy spectrum – from light to dark. Some people may find that what I have written is disturbing. I make no apologies for this. I want to give answers and explanations to some of the questions that I have been asked time and again. I believe passionately that knowledge should be shared. For too long, information about the dynamics of the spiritual world has remained behind the closed doors of many occult fraternities. I must state right away that the occult is not an area to be afraid of – it remains first and foremost a secret body of knowledge. The word itself stems from the Latin *'occultus'* which means, quite literally, clandestine or hidden. For most practicing occultists, the occult is simply a study of the deeper, spiritual 'reality' that extends beyond pure reason and the physical senses. But, as with everything in life, there is always a choice factor and in the occult, there is a choice to walk on the 'right hand' path (sometimes called white magic) or the 'left hand path' (referred to as black magic or satanism).

For the uninitiated, the head waters of occultism are as perilous a place to be as the open sea is to the inexperienced swimmer. Getting caught in a rip can be fatal. In the world of the occult, a little knowledge can be a dangerous thing and this is especially true in the current global climate of 'spirituality' where anything appears to go. Possession by demonic entities is a very real consequence for the 'dabbler' in the occult.

For some people it is through the realm of quantum physics that they become aware for the first time of the enormity of the vibrational reality we call home: our planet and every living thing on it. Yet despite passionate attempts by some of the world's leading scientists to harness the Higgs Particle, popularly known as the 'God Particle', science is nowhere near a final theory of physical reality.

My chief aim in composing the work that you are about to read is to open your eyes to the forces of nature, to the 'energy' that operates so powerfully in the universe. Although no one person will ever have all the answers and what today we hold as true may well be completely untrue many years later, I ask you to read this book with an open mind.

In the early years of my forays into the occult, I came across many 'healers' and 'energy workers' from the dark side whose chief aim was either to drain clients of their spiritual energy, thus empowering themselves, or simply to empty their wallets! I have also had occasion to encounter a number of ordinary looking 'humans' who were nothing less than full-blooded vampires (as opposed to the psychic vampires mentioned in this book) and have had my fair share of dealings with demonic entities of the darkest possible kind. I have seen, felt, heard and tasted many strange things that no séance room can disclose. I have kept vigil as the sun set below the horizon and the tides changed.

Throughout every single experience whether painful or exhilarating, I was learning all about the world of energy.

When you acknowledge and experience this amazing energy in the pure white light of being, it may well change your life, as it did mine.

'Seventy Thousand Veils' is about the *miracle of energy* – your energy, my energy, the earth's energy, and the universe's energy.

It is also an important guide to cleansing, healing and lifting negative human and atmospheric energy fields. It will offer vital insights to readers on three important areas: how *to live* happier, healthier lives; how *to slow down* and live at a more spiritual pace, and how *to free yourself to love unconditionally,* over coming self-doubt, truly knowing yourself, transforming disappointment and 'letting go' to love.

Sources of information on energy remain ancient religious texts, indigenous myths and legends (many from the mists of the past), the vast reservoir of traditional medicine which harnessed this energy (and still does, though most practitioners are today largely unaware of it) and last, though certainly not least, the hidden body of spiritual knowledge, which has come down to mankind through the centuries and of which modern contemporary society remains lamentably unaware – except in the guise of entertainment or 'get rich quick' schemes.

The title: *'Seventy Thousand Veils'* refers to the 70,000 veils of light and darkness that are said to swathe God, the ultimate source of all energy. According to The Koran, the Archangel Gabriel told the prophet Mohammed that if ever these veils were to be swept aside God would no longer exist.

When the great Elizabethan metaphysical poet and clergyman John Donne first wrote the incredible words: "no man is an island", he was talking about the fact that all mankind is connected. And it is connected - by this very energy via all of these 'veils'. Such vibration is the nucleus of all life in the universe and it is present in every living thing and every spiritual being.

We are linked by this non-material substance that, by its very nature, defies scientific measurement. Such energy moves through all of creation – even to places where oxygen cannot reach. Known to the Chinese as 'Chi' or breath of life, to the Japanese as 'Ki', even to the French as 'élan vital', this force has been the song of poets, dreamers and saints for centuries. It is glorious and luminescent and its existence has been recognized, respected and accepted by indigenous peoples for literally thousands of years. Only western man, caught up in the grip of the machine age, has lost the vision to see the footsteps in the sand....

Claire Porter, Melbourne, Australia.

PART ONE:

GENESIS – THE GATEWAY

THE BREATH OF GOD

"And the Lord God formed man of the dust of the ground, and breathed into his nostrils the breath of life: and the man became a living soul"
Genesis 2:9

Looking back, it was the press announcement that did it.

A few weeks before Christmas 2006, Professor Stephen Hawking told the British media that the human race must now move to another planet beyond our Solar System to protect the future of the species.

The much respected physicist and Cambridge academic, who shot to fame in the late 1980s with the publication of his book: "A Brief History of Time', was most insistent – the human race, he warned, could be wiped out by a nuclear disaster or an asteroid hitting the planet. Addressing his peers at a special ceremony prior to receiving the nation's top science award – the Royal Society's Copley Medal, Hawking stated that as there were no similar planets to Earth in our Solar System, humans would "have to go to another star". (1)

This brief statement was, for me as an experienced energy worker, nothing short of cathartic and led ultimately to the birth of this work,

For me, Hawking's reaction showed how infinitesimally small our knowledge actually is of this amazing planet and its many mysteries and his 'solution' for the human race is, in my opinion, no solution at all.

Over the face of the Earth lie literally thousands of intricate energy lines – they sweep through lush valleys, soar over majestic mountain ranges, course through rivers and great oceans and they resonate with the deeply spiritual voices of this our *only* and most unique world. Such energy is breath of our breath, light and darkness, water, air and food. It is infinite. It flows without ceasing. It is the energy of the entire universe. Without this mysterious substance all life on earth, as we know it, would perish.

In Hinduism and Buddhism, it is called simply *Prana.* To Christians, it is known as *Light.* To Russian researchers it has been labeled *Bioplasmic Energy.*

As the scientific fraternity grapples with learning more and more about less and less, it is becoming glaringly apparent that science itself can take us no further.

Man's destiny is linked inexorably with that of the earth. We are children of the cosmos, stuff of the stars. A microcosm of the macrocosm that is God. Our bodies vibrate to earth's radiant energies and electromagnetic charges. The very salts of the oceans run through our veins and when we depart this mortal life, all that remains of us are these 12 vital tissue salts – the Biochemical mineral salts so necessary for normal cell function and the maintenance of human health that were dynamized by Dr. Schuessler during the 19th century.

For all our proud knowledge of certain bodily processes such as the genetic code, the functioning of the nervous system, blood clotting, respiration and cellular activity, our knowledge base on *life itself remains largely superficial.* We know virtually next to nothing, for example, about basic life functions such as pain, sleep, memory, growth and healing. We are ignorant of nearly every single aspect of consciousness. The problem faced by western medicine of "when to pull the plug" shows that we don't even know for sure how to diagnose death!

Science attempts to deal with a subject – energy of life – that it does not fully understand, in spite of its bold claims of being able to do so. The dazzling application of Einstein's equation E = mc2 to show that matter can be created from energy, changed back into energy and subsequently altered by that energy, has been largely forgotten in a paroxysm of arrogance and smugness.

Our knowledge base on how this world came into being remains an hypothesis at best – in fact we know nothing more about Creation than did the ancient Greeks.

In terms of spiritual wisdom, we have reached an impasse, totally unable to learn from the lessons of our past history.

The miracle of energy continues to defy the narrow paradigms of scientific classification.

When I first learnt to dowse, I became acutely aware of the existence of this incredible energy – both positive and negative, of how energy fields on the earth and in the universe affect individual energy fields known as *auras*. I became aware of how psychic healers worked to both cleanse and to heal and of how, by being conscious of this energy and by using it in a positive way we can all reach out to discover peace of mind, extraordinary well being, joy at the heart centre, mental clarity and powerful inner strength. We can also use it to help heal the earth.

PRANA - ENERGY IN MOTION

As far as most people in the East are concerned, the presence of *Prana* is accepted without question. For them this force simply cannot be ignored or relegated to the realms of mysticism, the paranormal or even plain disbelief. For millions of Tibetans, Indians and Japanese 'faith healings' or 'miracle healings' are known as Pranic or Reiki healing and they are made possible by tapping into this amazing energy source. To most westerners, a miracle remains an act of God that science cannot explain. But for the average Tibetan, for example, that miracle is *Prana* – a Sanskrit word which means quite literally 'life giving force'.

As a Roman Catholic, I had been taught from early childhood to respect the power and majesty of God. It was not until many years later, as a dowser, that the Bible – both Old and New Testaments – became, for me, a completely different book. It is literally filled with both imagery and concrete instances of this energy or *Light* and its effect on mankind. The breath of God that gives birth to man in Genesis is the very first example of the transfer of this type of energy. During the birth, the public life and later, the crucifixion and the resurrection of Christ, the Son of God, there are numerous references to the potent energy of Jesus – His presence, the power of His words, the very touch of His garments. He is described by the Evangelist John as "the true light" of the world (John. Chpt.1:9-10).

About twenty-five hundred years ago, the wealthy son of a king near present day Nepal named Gotama, also experienced this energy. Weak and hungry from his constant wanderings and chosen life of austerity, the prince (disguised as a beggar) sat under the Banyan tree and meditated. What was the purpose of this life? If it was so impermanent, why then was it filled with so much uncertainty and suffering? In his extraordinary vision he saw men being born, he saw them suffering and dying, he followed their souls through the mysterious cycle of rebirth and death until he saw them return once more to the earth. We are told that the Prince seemed to "walk within the very hearts of men" until he could see and understand all of mankind's longings and desires. Later, when asked to sum up his teaching in a single word, Gotama said: "awareness". Today, to more than 300 million followers who tread the Eightfold Way to Enlightenment, this "awareness" is the essence of life itself. And this meditative state experience became a point of departure for the Prince who became the 29th Enlightened One, known as the Buddha – the "awakened one".

Incredible as it may seem, this same energy is used by us all for every single thought, word and deed each and every day. It is restored every time we breathe. It leaves us only at death, when it begins another journey towards another energetic entity, as the Tibetan missive 'The Bardo of Death' (Book of Death) reminds us. Such energy can be used to benefit mankind, or to harm it.

It is very, very powerful.

THE ENERGIES OF THE EARTH

The world around us vibrates to this energy too.

Sinuous and mercurial by nature, earth energies fluctuate and change with sunrise and sunset, with the waxing and the waning of the moon, with the passing of the sun through the seasons and throughout the deep, still cycles of planetary time. Indigenous cultures were keenly aware of the seasonal rise and fall of this land energy, of where its most powerful nodal points could be found, and the times at which the energy at these places would be most active and could be tapped. The great standing stones and circles that pepper the landscape of northern Europe, the pyramids of Egypt, the temples of ancient Greece, the sacred Mayan and Incan sites in the Americas and the great stone statutes of Easter Island – all are evidence of ancient man's attempts to both tap into these energy fields, to pin them down and to harness their special powers throughout the year.

The respect with which our ancestors treated this 'spirit of place' is also demonstrated by their refusal to touch certain areas – many places were simply left untouched by nomadic peoples and these centers continued to ebb and flow with elemental forces that can still be felt today. The great spaces, rarefied air and height of the mountain ranges in Tibet and the pervading silence where men are scarce and wildlife scarcer still is a power-point for such energy. Ayres Rock in Australia is another. Standing at the heart of the red centre of the continent and rising majestically out of the sands of the desert – a beacon of life for hundreds of miles around – it is a clear example of sacred land. So too are the burial grounds of Native American Red Indians. Who, among us, can remain untouched by the sheer magnetism of these places?

A DOWSER COMETH

But what exactly is this channeling universal life energy and how does it work?

With the explosion of interest in matters related to Mind-

Body-Spirit, so many words have been written and even more spoken on "energy" – energy healing, energy vibrations, the healing sounds of music – even the "power" that emanates from simply being yourself and of allowing your own positive consciousness full rein!

Yet, all of these things are merely *aspects* of Prana. Prana is *both* consciousness and unconsciousness, it is simultaneously positive and negative, it manifests as physical, while *at the same time,* it is quintessentially spiritual.

Confused? Let me explain.

My first "tangible" experience of Prana was somewhat of a shock.

It occurred when I was six months pregnant with my third child. Faced with the needs of a growing family (the twins were now four years of age), the move to larger home with more bedrooms and a garden had become a priority. But, house hunting was proving to be both an exhausting and intensive process and for many months it seemed as if we should never find the perfect family home – for us, anyway. One afternoon, we stumbled, quite by chance, on a property that seemed (on paper and from the outside at least) a reasonable proposition. An inspection was duly arranged with the local real estate agent and, at the appointed time, we viewed the house.

It was a large rambling California bungalow set high on a hill, surrounded by a lush and exquisite garden in a leafy Melbourne suburb.

From the moment I set foot inside the front door, I began to feel uneasy. This feeling grew on me the further inside the house I went. By the time I reached the formal lounge, I felt really unwell – nauseous and breathless. It was a typical Australian mid-summer's day – 30 degrees in the shade, but I started shivering. My eldest daughter tugged at my hand and asked: "Why are you so cold, mummy?"

Her twin chimed in: "Mummy's gone all wobbly."

I had started to shake. The floor on which I was standing felt like a block of ice and I couldn't move.

I interrupted the real estate agent's sales patter: "Something has happened in this house."

My husband and the agent just stared at me and, to my astonishment the estate agent actually blushed and then started stammering. I repeated my statement (a little bit more gently this time) and, with a sigh, the agent told us the "history" of the house.

The property had been owned by a returned serviceman and his wife. They had lived in the house since the husband's return from the Far East where he had been a POW of the Japanese. The couple had had one child, a daughter, the sole heir to the property and who was now residing in Perth, Western Australia. The estate agent insisted that: "It had been a happy house – a *very* happy house". But, unfortunately, the couple had died suddenly of massive heart attacks within minutes of each other and they had lain, undiscovered, in the lounge room (on the very spot where I was standing) for *three weeks.*

Needless to say, we did not purchase the property. As a young woman I had no idea of how to clear this stuck energy and release the earthbound spirits of these deceased individuals. We decided to continue with our house hunting. Later, however, we learnt that the property had been purchased shortly afterwards by a young married couple who wanted to start a family. On a Sunday afternoon drive a year (and a new house) later, my husband suddenly thought it would be a "nice idea" to see what had become of the "haunted house". It had been beautifully renovated and *it was for sale once more.*

As a novice dowser, I became aware that this experience was a prime example of Prana in action – my spiritual body had made a connection with this extraordinary energy. My physical body (the heavily pregnant me with my symptoms of nausea and severe cold) had felt this exchange. My spirit had touched the spirits of the serviceman and his wife and had felt their confusion and inability to accept the state of death. It is my sincere hope that they have since been released....

Hospitals have the same affect on me. Within a short time of entering them, I become physically unwell and actually start vomiting - sometimes, I cannot even get past the reception area! During a visit to a leading hospital in Melbourne a few years ago the energies of the building were so intense that the further inside I ventured, the worse I began to feel. As we approached the wards, I began to feel as if I was suffocating and I started to experience severe stomach cramps. Being acutely sensitive to energy fields, I had no alternative but to leave the building. As soon as we had done so, I began to throw up – violently, my energy levels were very low and I knew that I had walked into an area of extremely negative energy. When we had crossed the road, I looked up at the building. It was summer and the street was bathed in brilliant sunlight, yet the hospital was in darkness. I knew that some very barbaric things had been done in that place and if ever a building was haunted by the ghosts of those who had died needlessly within its walls, this was definitely the place. To this day, I cannot even drive past this building without feeling unwell. As a point of interest, it is no co-incidence that all hospitals are built over large bodies of negative water – but more of this later...

CHANGE YOUR THINKING & YOU CHANGE YOUR LIFE

We are actually born *with two bodies: the physical shell and the spiritual or subtle shell.*

Pranic energy flows through this spiritual body and is connected to the physical body at the navel through a tiny link. When this thin silver cord is cut, Prana is severed, the physical and spiritual bodies then separate and death occurs. The radiance of Prana is then absorbed back into the subtle body and the great cycle of life starts once more as the soul of the departed seeks to be reincarnated into another physical shell in the endless cycle of existence from one rebirth to the next, known to Buddhists as *Samsara.*

While the physical body is merely the densest and most visible level of energetic matter, eastern tradition – whether Ayurvedic or Tibetan – holds that the spiritual body is bathed in many levels of energetic matter. Although the energy body follows the contours of the physical body, it is much larger than the physical shell. It is transparent, luminous and highly colorful and is charged with subtle frequencies. Its layers comprise the etheric, astral and mental (containing instinctive, intellectual and spiritual sub-levels) as well as the pure spirit or causal. Each of these fields or *auras* interacts with the other and together, these high frequency energy bodies combine to stimulate the creation of the physical body. It has even been suggested that this spiritual or energetic organization occurs *before* the manifestation of the physical matrix we call the human body through which this amazing energy, Prana, now flows.

While prayer, or meditation, remains the purest form of Prana, thoughts are the most powerful. In this context, the motto: "change your thinking and you change your life", is especially valid. Such consciousness is Prana in motion. Alternatively, Einstein's other theory, which states that: "You cannot solve a problem with the same mind that created it", displays an unwillingness to alter a mindset and is a good indicator of a blockage in the flow of Prana. Such blockages usually manifest in physical symptoms of later ill health.

WHY SOME PEOPLE HEAL & OTHERS DON'T

And this, of course, is why some people heal, while others do not.

According to author Louise L. Hay cancer is caused by constant negativity that has been bottled up inside a person for years. By not expressing ourselves, by not allowing our 'true' emotions of love, peace and happiness to flow, Hay maintains that we become sick.

When I examine ill health from the perspective of energy work, I find that cancer, for example, usually comes at the end of a long road of specific causes. In most cases, it manifests *within the spiritual body first and is subsequently a failure of the physical body to regulate its own metabolism and stimulate correct immune responses.*

The case of a young man whose mother was dying of a brain tumor is especially revealing. A colleague of mine had been called to a house to measure and correct the energy lines to the property. Although he could locate no significant negativity either on the land or in the home, what he did find was that both the bedrooms of the mother and her son were beside each other, *but that the bed heads of each shared the same dividing wall.* It soon became clear what was happening. At nights, while the son slept his powerful negative thoughts were released and absorbed by his unsuspecting, but acutely sensitive mother. As the years wore on, the woman's health began to deteriorate to the extent that her crown charka had started to close. When the energy flow to this spiritual high point is either blocked or tapped, the victim can become 'disconnected' from the world and headaches and memory problems can initially result. As this chakra is linked to the pineal gland, the person affected may experience sleeping problems, neurological disorders, even seizures. The cerebral cortex can also be affected. The answer was quite simple – the son was given some helpful advice on releasing safely the pent up anger he had a habit of accumulating and both beds were moved. The mother soon made a complete recovery to the bafflement of her medical practitioner.

Of course, the pressures of modern life also play a large part in ill health. Often people get sick because they push themselves to the limit, stressing and abusing their bodies. Most people, I have found, really do not love themselves. In fact, we are taught that to listen to our innermost thoughts, to care for ourselves and even to 'honour' the type of person we would really like to be is *selfish!* We spend so long trying to please other people that we can end up feeling resentful, hurt and often angry. And this, of course, is when sickness starts...

But if anger is destructive, it can also be liberating. For only anger can show us what is really wrong with our lives. Anger is precious because it can become a teacher, a guide to pranic blockages and a way through the pain...

When anger is finally released, it is often replaced rapidly by fear (fear that the cancer, for example, may come back etc.). Once fear has been eliminated, self-pity is the third and final stage on the path to wellness. When a disease has been removed, I often find that the person concerned almost always goes through a period of 'missing' their respective illness. It is a sad but true fact that many an invalid 'identifies' themselves by their illness. When the 'disease' is no longer there, it can create real problems for some individuals – on a purely practical level, government support may cease; on an emotional level, there is the fear that people will stop treating them in a special way or could even become demanding of them. As incredible as it seems, the recovering person invariably begins a cycle of self-pity! But, once this sentiment has been surrendered, the individual is well and truly on the road to improved health.

When I listen to people talking, I often get a good indication of health status.

Speech itself resonates with Prana – especially when it is filled with love and gratitude as Masaro Emoto found out in one of his early experiments with water crystals. When a group of people were asked to project these positive sentiments onto water samples, the crystalline structures of the water specimens revealed stunningly beautiful jewel-like forms and intricate shapes. Water exposed to "thank-you" formed enchanting hexagonal crystals, but other samples that had been labeled with words such as "you fool" and commands such as "Do it!" reflected ugly forms, colors and shapes. These crystals were malformed and fragmented. Music vibrations had the same effect on water crystals – especially the graceful classical music of Mozart or Beethoven's moving Pastoral Symphony about the coming of spring to the world. When played over the water samples, this music resulted in delicate lace-like and elegant shapes. Violent heavy-metal music however resulted in fragmented and malformed water crystals! As the human body is more than 70% water and the surface of the earth is primarily that of ocean, it should come as no surprise to find that water has the ability to register and to remember these Pranic vibrations whether spoken or written, or conveyed in thought-forms, feelings or sound. (2)

The message is clear – when we manifest positive, loving thoughts we grow spiritually (and physically). But, when we choose to believe negative things about other people and ourselves – when we live on a "diet" of toxic emotions and actions, our energy shrinks, slows down and eventually stops. And this is when disease takes hold.

THE HUMAN ENERGY FIELD

The pathways or bioplasmic lines along which Prana runs are called *Meridians* (in China – the same channels that are used in acupuncture) or *Nadis* (in India). At specific points along this energy field, concentrations of Prana occur. These points are called *Chakras.*

Put simply, a chakra is a whirling vortex of energy at the conjunction point of the mind and the body. Chakras are present in the etheric body and resemble spinning wheels as Pranic energy tends to course through them in a spiral fashion – much like that of the firework, the catherine wheel.

Ancient Indian texts suggest that there are a myriad of minor chakras that directly access the cellular structure of the physical body – as well as the seven major chakra vortices. These seven chakras are connected on the energy plane with the function of the principal body organs and are associated with a particular gland of the endocrine system, giving access to the hormonal flows and changes in the body. They are also intimately connected to the body's central nervous system.

All of your senses, all of your perceptions and possible states of awareness – in short, everything that you can possibly experience, can be divided up into seven categories. Each category can then be associated with a particular charka. Not only do chakras mirror particular aspects of the physical body, they also represent parts of your consciousness.

When you feel tension in your consciousness, you actually feel it in the chakra linked to that part of your consciousness experiencing the stress and in the physical body organ associated with that chakra. In this context, *where* you feel the stress, depends on *why* you feel the stress. Tension in the chakra is detected by the nerves of the plexus associated with that chakra and is then transmitted to the parts of the body controlled by that plexus. When the tension continues over a period of time, or is magnified in intensity, the individual creates a symptom on the personal level. I thought it especially interesting when former British Prime Minister, Tony Blair, had to have a minor operation to correct a long-standing fault with his heart a few years back. When viewed from the Pranic perspective, the heart chakra represents the body's joy centre. It is quite literally, the 'heart' for unconditional love – including self-love and is the focal point for the thymus gland, which is the key to our immune system. When we manifest joy in our lives, our hearts are healthy. We are, quite literally, happy with our lives....

When a person makes significant changes for the better, the symptom has no further reason for being and can be released according to whatever he or she allows themselves to believe is possible.

An understanding of how Prana works – via the relationship between the spiritual and the physical – and learning how to control the flow of prana throughout *makes everything in the universe possible.* When you have attained this level of understanding, *anything can be healed. Anything.*

In so many ways and often without our conscious awareness, we feel the presence of Prana in our lives every day.

When two people who care about one another, hug each other, Pranic energy literally explodes and can be felt very clearly by both parties. Through lovemaking, Prana is exchanged at the most intimate level. The love of a mother for her child knows no bounds and the mother gives freely of her energy to the tiny infant. We even describe those with the "gift of the gab" as having the "power of persuasion" – but what is this really, except the ability to wield Pranic power?

The greatest energy transfer of all remains that of spiritual masters. In numerous paintings, this energy is represented by the *halo* – the beacon of light that surrounds the heads of such people. After the resurrection, Jesus, we are told, radiated with this bright light, as did the apostles and, later on, the saints. Those among us who have seen angels quite often refer to them as "crystal beings" or "beings of Divine Light" – their luminosity is so dazzling. Haloes can be seen on statues and paintings of the Buddha and other eastern deities with the Jewish mystical teaching, the Kabbalah, referring to this energy as *astral light.*

During Near Death Experiences (NDE), Pranic light and sound can be seen and heard very clearly.

NEAR DEATH EXPERIENCES

On September 17th, 1975, US author Dannion Brinkley was talking on the telephone during a thunderstorm when a bolt of lightning hit the phone line. Thousands of volts of electricity surged instantly though Brinkley's head and down his body, throwing him several feet into the air. His heart stopped and he died.

When Brinkley was revived in the morgue *after twenty-eight minutes*, he had an incredible story to tell.

After the lightening strike, Brinkley watched from above as loved ones and doctors worked frantically to restart his heart. As his spirit hovered over his body, he had his first glimpse of human auras. He afterwards described these energy fields as displaying radiant, multi-faceted and jewel-like hues and colors. As he watched, he saw his loved ones' auras change sharply from deep red to orange as they experienced feelings of complete despair and utter frustration. When medics proclaimed him dead, Brinkley was already travelling through a dark tunnel towards a spirit being, who led him into a crystal city awash in incredible light and tranquility. There, he said, he beheld "the most magnificent sight of all". Brought before 13 angelic instructors in what he describes as "a cathedral of knowledge", Brinkley was told of events that would shake the world before the year 2000 – including the Chernobyl nuclear disaster and the Persian Gulf War.

In his amazing book "Saved by The Light", Brinkley remarked that these Beings of Light were so exquisitely luminous because of their auras. He later commented: "As we grow spiritually and advance in our capacity to love unconditionally, our aura intensifies and expands in direct proportion". (3)

Yet, despite their fervent denials of the possibility that man is much more than a mere physical being, some members of the scientific fraternity remain fascinated by the human mind-body-spirit link. One of the most important breakthroughs in scientific understanding of MBS has come through the development of high-frequency photography, better known today as *Kirlian photography*.

The process was first developed by Semyon Kirlian in Russia in the early years of the 20th century. His electrotherapy of living objects revealed multi-colored flares, sparks and flashes radiating outward from the object. The electrical pattern changed from one time to another depending on influencing conditions. Leaves severed from a plant, for example, showed a deteriorating energy field and diseased leaves produced different colors and patterns to healthy ones.

Of greater importance to medical science though was Kirlian's discovery that photographs of his fingers were different when he was ill. The pictures were blurred and the colors less distinct than when well. He also learned that emotional states, such as excitement or anger, altered these energy patterns.

Today, further tests have indicated that a stressful condition (eg: cancer) is revealed in the aura long before it becomes manifest in the physical body and that the energy fields of healers influence the energy field of the recipient. Dr. Thelma Moss at UCLA, and several other scientists, has since used high-frequency photography to measure the difference in energy patterns of healers before, during and after a healing session. The pictures revealed a building up of energy in the hands and then a transfer of some of this energy to the patient. After the treatment, the healer's hands have less and the patient more of this energy field.

Of course, the major critics of faith healing claim that the healing takes place not because the healer has done anything – but because the recipient believes himself to be healed. While a change in attitude and the acceptance by the patient of being in a state of wellness as opposed to illness does play a significant role in healthcare, all of the scientific results to date indicate that there is so much more to healing than mere psychology.

The healing power of prayer in particular continues to defy the time-worn concept of man as mechanical being.

In recent years, intercessory prayer (praying for someone else) has been studied as a healing tool by major US hospitals. The results are simply amazing. When many of her patients with advanced AIDS reported that they were getting benefit from prayer and spiritual healers, Dr. Barbara Tang, psychiatrist and

Director of the Complementary Medicine Research Institute at California Pacific Medical Centre in San Francisco, decided to study *distant healing*. She set up a study in which half of her patients were prayed for by spiritual healers from a wide range of traditions – including Buddhist, Native American, Jewish, Christian and shamanic. The healers were told the first names and symptoms of the patients. They were also given a photo of each patient. Family and medical staff did not know who was being prayed for – only the researchers.

After six months, the patients who were prayed for had significantly fewer new AIDS-defining illnesses. They had spent fewer days in hospital and had needed to see their doctors less often. In addition to this, they also showed a boost in their overall mood. *Not one of the patients knew they were being prayed for.*

Prayer has not only a profound effect on the recipient; it also lifts the person praying to a place where the light is golden, warm and ever gentle. Praying is good for you, your aura expands and your vibrations are lifted to a higher, spiritual plane.

LEY LINES

But, just as our bodies reflect the miracle of Prana, so too does the earth.

Everything that is contained within our spiritual bodies (meridians and chakras) is also mirrored in the anatomy of the earth's subtle body. We have meridians, chakras and auras – but the planet too has an auric 'skin' with its own network of meridians and chakras. Mother Earth is literally teeming with spiritual life.

When he was working on his book 'The Galaxy on Earth: A Traveler's Guide to the Planet's Visionary Geography', US author Richard Leviton made an astonishing discovery. (4) While researching the extraterrestrial nature of the earth, he noticed that the abundance of sacred sites on the planet is actually *distributed uniformly around the globe and that, when seen as a whole, they appear to express a pattern that is an edited, condensed version of the entire galaxy.* In all, Leviton surmised that about 57,000 stars are represented across the surface of the planet and that these stars correspond *directly and immediately* to the many thousands of holy places that are dotted across the world.

A spiritualized conception of the galaxy via this sacred sites matrix is however only one feature among many in the earth's energy body.

The study of *Geomancy* - which literally means the divination *(mantos)* of the energy and conscious secrets of the earth *(Ge)* - has done much to alter our way of thinking in regard to the practice of reading and relating to the delicate energies of the earth. This study lies at the core of the relationship that all cultures have had with the environment since time began. The geomantic awareness of indigenous peoples everywhere – be they Celts, Inuit or Australian Aboriginals – was woven into tribal social, political and economic fabrics. These cultures sought out and actively engaged in intimate relationships with power centers, holy places and sacred rivers. With the dawning of the Reformation, when popular mass consciousness was evolving paving the way for the Age of Reason and later, the industrialization of society, Geomancy faded from the European landscape. But it has recently experienced resurgence in the form of Feng Shui, the ancient Chinese version of geomancy, which stemmed from the imperial culture of China.

For centuries, these sacred sites or *Power Centers* remained the original destination of pilgrims. They represented a point of contact and functioned rather like umbilical cords – feeding and nourishing the spirit of an individual, a community or even an entire culture. Shrines, temples and later on, churches were frequently built over such places.

From the energetic standpoint, whenever a place has had prayers or human energy (via rites or rituals) directed at it, that place then becomes a vortex of cosmic, vibrating electricity. It becomes site of much force – a life force that can be used by those who are sensitive for great good or great evil.

The old walled city of Jerusalem is one of the most significant Power Centres on the earth. A veritable crossroads of spiritual energy, the city itself lies at the core of Jewish, Christian and Islamic prayers. Its sacred places – the holy stones, the Church of the Sepulcher, the Wailing Wall, The Garden of Gethsemane – have absorbed people's prayers and spiritual energy for thousands of years. It is said that Heaven and Earth truly meet in Jerusalem and the existence of the 'Jerusalem Syndrome', where tourists are visibly touched by the presence of God, is a well recognized syndrome. It is then no coincidence to discover that the city is situated on a unique energy vortex that can be communicated with while dowsing with L-rods.

Glastonbury too is of special interest. This little English market town, so steeped in history, is the mystical site of King Arthur's Avalon and the nucleus of the Grail legend. It is a truly extraordinary place where aspects of paganism, the early Christian Church and a wide variety of other spiritual beliefs and philosophies co-exist in harmony. The town has been a centre of pilgrimage for 10,000 years and it is no co-incidence that twin *Ley Lines* gather and concentrate with tremendous strength on Glastonbury. You can feel the spiritual electricity in the air. Known as the "Michael and Mary" lines that run all the way from Cornwall to Norfolk, these leys weave through Glastonbury with concentrated force – Glastonbury Abbey, the tor and the famous Avebury stone circle are swathed in their energy.

For many years, it was assumed that Leys were merely ancient tracks created in the distant past by our tribal ancestors.

But to dowsers leys are more than just old walkways. They are routes of powerful energy that concentrate and redirect *potent earth energies enabling people to live in fulfillment and plenty. They are myriad strands of connection that are distributed across the face of the earth.*

Almost totally forgotten, they were rediscovered in 1921 by Alfred Watkins, a respected Herefordshire businessman, who while looking at a map for features of interest noticed a straight line that passed over hilltops through various points of interest – all of which were ancient. At the time of his discovery, Watkins had no theories about alignments but on that June afternoon, he saw "in a flash" a whole pattern of lines stretching across the landscape. Four years later in 1925, he published his findings in a book: 'The Old Straight Track' and the British public learnt that ancient mounds, prehistoric earthworks, standing stones and old moats and churches seemed to fall in dead straight alignments *on these very lines.* At Stonehenge, arguably Europe's most famous cult site, 12 such energy lines are said to converge. Watkins chose to call these alignments 'Leys' because of the frequency with which the Saxon place name had occurred along them. In some places these leys even overlaid stretches of ancient straight roads and trackways. Although Watkins may not have fully recognized what he saw at the time, leys remain powerful energy grids and it is no coincidence that such sacred monuments were erected on them. To this day, every single Christian Church is built on a Ley Line. Coincidence? I don't think so. The energy picture becomes even more intriguing when we discover that many of today's *crop circles* have appeared in the immediate vicinity of prehistoric structures and sites and within the same radius of these lines.

Dowsing bridges the gap between rational and intuitive and gives us potentially unlimited access to this information about a world of which we are indeed an integral part. As a dowser, I find these energy lines fascinating and am constantly amazed at the sheer power and strength of their vibrations and their affect on people living unknowingly close to them. But the picture becomes even more intriguing with the discovery of these channels elsewhere in the world.

At Nazca in Peru, dead straight lines were marked out for miles on the dusty grey and very flat desert plain by ancient tribal people. On a trip to the area some years ago, I was astonished to find that these lines were ritually swept by local people and that this practice is still carried out today, though in a more Christian context. As they stretch for 500 square kilometers (193 square miles), this is no mean feat. Some of the lines connect burial places, are associated with ancestor cults and were known from folk tradition to have been the routes of spirits. Many hypotheses about their real purpose have been put forward, the most famous of which is, arguably, Erich Von Daniken's theory so painstaking set out in 'Chariots of the Gods'. In it, Von Daniken set out to prove that these lines represented landing strips for beings from outer space. Although he postulated that these beings were Extra Terrestrials, is it not also possible that they may have been connection points for spiritual entities like angels? The unusual headgear seen on ancient murals look to me strangely like haloes as opposed to the helmets of astronauts - but more of this later in the book.

When we travelled to Bolivia, we found the existence of similar straight paths high up in the altiplano. They ran unchallenged for miles through the most hostile terrain. Further investigation revealed that the Bolivian tracks stretched from prominent hills and mountains to isolated shrines (all now Christianized) – just like Watkins' ley lines in England. It is also perhaps no coincidence that the local Bolivians view the mountains and hills as the dwelling places of spirits.

The much more recent discovery of ritual roads in New Mexico via infra-red satellite photography gives us even more food for thought. Barely visible at ground level, these roads run straight out from Chaco Canyon on whose floor lie the ruins of ancient settlements and sacred buildings known as kivas. The roads appear to have been made by clearing surface stones and piling them in berms alongside the routes. While some of the roads run parallel to one another, others seem to go nowhere, simply petering out into the desert – all of which would suggest that transport was not the primary function of these roads. As the indigenous people, the Anasazi, did not have either the wheel or the horse, the reason for the building of this carefully planned network becomes even more intriguing.

In the land of my parents, Ireland, invisible fairy passes run in straight lines between fairy forts or raths and circular earth-works of known antiquity. As a child on family holidays I was fascinated by the stories that my grandmother used to tell us about the 'little people' who could be seen by some dancing on the banks of these forts as anthromorphs radiant and beautiful with rays of colored lights streaming from them. It was considered to be very bad luck to block a fairy pass and woe betide the man who cut down a fairy tree! The Irish government learnt just such a lesson in the 1980s when it attempted to do just this while building a major road through a locally respected fairy area. In the end, the road was detoured around the now famous tree. There are, of course those who profess that much of this spirit geography exists only in the folk mind, but some of these ancient routes have in fact been overlaid by straight roads. As the Romans never reached Ireland, these channels were allowed to flow freely through the landscape for centuries. The ancient Newgrange monument, which stands at nearly 11 meters high and almost 90 meters in diameter, was built more than 5,000 years ago by people whose tools came from the very rocks in which the stones were hewn. On December 21st each year, the sun's rays penetrate the full length of the tunnel and illuminate the furthest reaches of its intricately decorated walls. For precisely 17 minutes on this one day in the year, the spirits of the departed are awakened. But perhaps the most amazing aspect of Newgrange is the undeniable fact that these ancient Celts had grasped the mathematics and physics required to manufacture an opening in the exact position above the entrance to the passageway so that as the sun rose on this special day, its life-giving energy could be tapped for spiritual use.

Elsewhere in northern Europe we find the existence of long stretches of straightish lines aligned to Neolithic long barrows and the link with death and ritual. Stone rows and avenues, Viking cult roads and in Holland the medieval doodwegen or death roads still survive in the landscape and it was along these roads that the dead were carried to a burial ground. Documentary evidence even shows that in some areas it was against the law to carry a corpse on another route – the route to the spirit world had to be straight.

In China we once again meet the connection between straightness, spirits and the dead. In imperial times, straight lines in the landscape were considered unlucky and were avoided at all costs – except where the divine influence of the Emperor was concerned. Malign spirits were believed to travel along straight paths and good luck could be drained from a site along a straight route. It should be remembered that the original focus of Feng Shui was the auspicious location of tombs.

Elsewhere in the world, we find the existence of the great pyramids in Egypt (once again connected with death) on straight lines and sited directly on leys.

The Kogi Indians of Columbia, who inhabit a remote mountainous region, have managed to preserve many of their traditional beliefs and way of life despite the 16th century Spanish invaders and the more pervasive spread of contemporary Western culture. These people were the subject of an evocative film by Alan Ereira in 1990. In the film, Ereira was shown the map stone, a megalith criss-crossed with straight grooves which he was told was a map of physical roads in the region. *In addition, the map stone showed the location of invisible routes which existed only in the spirit world and which were travelled by a class of Kogi adepts known as mamas who looked after the spiritual well-being of their people.* A large part of Kogi cosmology involves shamanic travel and complex traditional practices designed to maintain ecological balance in the environment. This is still a living tradition.

The link that we have been looking for amongst all of these places is, of course, spirit travel.

Neurologically, the straightness comes from the entopic nature of the out-of-body or NDE. Spirals, zig-zags, lines, lattices or the tunnel motif can all be seen on these ancient monuments that have been built on very precise points around the planet. Their existence – and that of the spiritual world – cannot be denied. What Watkins stumbled upon all those years ago were the remains of arterial and archaic spirit lines that map the globe. The resemblance between them and the meridians of the spiritual body along which Prana flows is now very obvious.

SPIRIT ATTACHMENT

As our physical bodies return to the earth, our subtle energetic body seeks to move to another plane of existence. Sometimes this is achieved with relative ease and often with help from the living, as the existence of these ley lines serves to demonstrate. But there are occasions when this energy cannot move on and becomes 'stuck'. This condition is reflected through various etheric energy fields on the earth and is known as *Geopathic stress.*

Technically speaking Geopathic stress is best considered as a dysfunction in the relationship between person and place. It has two main causes.

The first is when we spend extended periods of time in etheric energy fields which, by their very nature, are simply NOT conducive to human health. There are indeed places on the planet where man should not go. The Chinese call these paths *yin-chi* which through their very nature absorb, drain and deplete our subtle energies. At a mental level, when exposed to these areas, we can experience fatigue, poor concentration, impaired communication and a reduced tolerance towards any kind of stressful or challenging situation. At an emotional level, we can feel low in spirits and tend to withdraw from society. Also, it is not uncommon for the body's natural hormonal cycles to be disturbed. The Chinese believe that if a building is constructed on an imbalanced or yin-chi path, it will remain unhealthy unless the basic nature of the energy present can be reconfigured.

The second case of Geopathic stress is when an otherwise healthy and flourishing energy field becomes stressed and traumatized and the flow of Prana or Chi is disturbed, blocked or out of harmony.

Sometimes this is the result of physical traumatic changes to the landscape such as quarrying or new construction projects. But more often than not, when a place becomes traumatized, it is the direct consequence of intense and emotionally disturbing human activity. An example of this is the former Auschwitz concentration camp. It is a little known fact that birds, for example, will not fly over the site because of the deep negative energy that continues to exist there as a result of the appalling human atrocities. Birds are acutely sensitive to magnetic energy fields and are often among the first animal species to detect vibrational changes in the environment.

The most classic example of environmental trauma however remains battlefields where much human blood has been shed.

The earth holds a memory of these happenings and similar events can even occur in a repeating fashion in that same location as people's energies resonate with the etheric fields – both charging one another with the thoughts and feelings held there. The Omaha beachhead near Point du Hoc and Trevieres in northern Normandy, France, was the scene of one of the major D-Day landings of World War II. On this wind-swept beach more than 6,000 allied troops were either wounded, declared missing in action or killed within 24 hours. To this very day the beach remains an eerie and desolate place filled with the energies of stuck spirits. 'Ground Zero' in New York is, unfortunately, another such place.

Environments like these that have witnessed such great tragedies are not healthy for further human habitation until the energy at these levels has been cleared and rebalanced. Only then can many unhappy and confused spirits truly go to the Light.

It is always possible to enter into a creative dialogue with the spirit of these places and to lift the blocked, stagnant or overly stimulated chi paths running through the space.

I remember the case of Betty, a farmer's wife from rural Victoria who experienced a very alarming case of this kind.

Shortly after Betty and her husband had retired to a smaller holding, they began to notice odd things about their new home. As Betty spent more time inside the house, she became more receptive to these changes. When she sat on an armchair in the lounge room she gradually became filled with most intense sadness. When she moved the chair to another spot, this did not happen.

As time marched on though, Betty found that every time she entered the room this profound feeling of melancholy would sweep over her once more. Being of a curious mind, she set out to study the history of the house and to her great surprise, newspaper reports from the 1920s at the regional library revealed that a young newly-married woman had been brutally murdered by her husband in a former house on the very land that Betty and her husband now occupied. As houses tend to be built on the same block and almost always on the same spot for utility connection purposes, it did not take Betty long to put two and two together.

An exorcism was duly arranged via Betty's local parish priest – and for a while all seemed well, but gradually these feelings of grief returned only this time the entire room began to get very cold.

Several healers were recruited in an attempt to shift this

energy – some tried and failed, others simply refused to help. By the time Don arrived, Betty had had enough and was getting ready to relocate.

After a stroll all over the inside and outside of the house, Don told her that he didn't think that he could help her as the energy was so strong, but that he was willing to "give it a go".

Gathering four large rocks from the fields surrounding the property, Don placed one at each corner of the house. Then, taking two smaller stones, he entered the lounge room, knelt down on the 'infected' spot and started praying. When he had finished, he began banging the two rocks together. He kept this up in a regular, rhythmic pace for a good twenty minutes then began clashing the rocks furiously against one another and imploring the entity to "seek the light". A suddenly as he had started, Don stopped. The stuck energy of the traumatized young woman had at last been released from the land nearly half a century later and the house was now at peace as well.

EVIL ENERGY - BEHIND THE VEIL OF DARKNESS

Unfortunately, no book on energy would be complete without mention of the more negative aspects of Prana. At this stage, I would like to point out that while Prana is in itself essentially good, there have been (as we have just read), still are and will continue to be certain individuals who will attempt to manipulate this life force for their own evil purposes.

Albert Speer, Hitler's architect, was very clearly interested in geomancy, leys and other sacred spots throughout Germany and some of his architecture betrays definite knowledge of the basic principles of geomancy. The *Vril Society,* an esoteric group, promoted the idea that there might be a mystical energy within the earth that could be tapped by the German people. It is well known that Hitler employed dowsers on the battlefield to search for water and minefields and that Nazi scientists displayed intense interest in 'free energy' devices. The search by the Reich for the Holy Grail and the Ark of the Covenant were clearly representative of the pursuit of a path to transcendent consciousness.

When Hitler annexed Austria one of his first official acts was to drive to the Hapsburg Treasure House in Vienna in a motorcade and claim the Spear of Destiny. Known more correctly as the Spear of Longinus, the weapon, which pierced the side of Christ, this solitary iron spearhead, had once been in the possession of the Holy Roman Emperor Charlemagne and had been demanded by Napoleon after his victory over Austria at the battle of Austerlitz in 1805.

Before his rise to power, Hitler was a penniless and despairing artist who often used to spend afternoons inside the Hapsburg Treasure House where he knew he would find warmth and shelter against the harshness of the weather. One day, absorbed with his own thoughts about the hopelessness of his personal plight, Hitler claims that he hardly noticed an official party moving around the exhibits under the guidance of a museum expert. The group stopped almost in front of him, while their guide pointed to an ancient spearhead. Later in 'Mein Kampf' Hitler described his feelings: " And then I heard the words that were to change my whole life: 'There is a legend associated with this Spear that whoever claims it, and solves its secrets, *holds the destiny of the world in his hands for good or evil'*.... The Spear appeared to be some sort of magical medium of revelation for it brought the world of ideas into such close and living perspective that human imagination became more real than the world of sense. I felt as though I myself had held it in my hands before in some earlier century of history".

This talisman of omnipotence and goodness is said to possess the power to overcome all odds and conquer the world. On that fateful day at the Weltliche Schatzkammer as a young Adolf Hitler dreamed a dream, World War II became inevitable. A new age and a New World order steered by the Third Reich was waiting to happen....The dropout who slept in flophouses was to become the 'chosen one', the Führer, leader of one of the most evil cults the world has ever known and whose legacy of cloning, genetic engineering and nuclear weaponry is very much alive and well in the world today...

The most insidious form of dark energy manipulation is known as *psychic attack.*

Much has been written on the subject and there are those who claim that negative energies, entities and psychic attacks do not exist and cannot happen if you refuse to believe in them or give them energy by paying attention to them. Sadly, this is simply not the case. Problems can and do happen as a result of negative energies and psychic attacks. At the very least they can leave you feeling drained and exhausted, at their worst, they can kill you. There is no easy way to say this.

The phenomenon of Harry Potter, the boy wizard, and his adventures for example, have not just been pure entertainment. Many parents and church leaders from Europe, the US as well as throughout Australia and New Zealand have voiced their concerns about children trying to emulate the book's hero by dabbling in bits of black magic. Many of these people now want to know how they can help their teenagers. There are disadvantages as well as advantages to delving too deeply into the Potter books, as we shall discover much later on.

It has been well over half a century since British-born occultist Dion Fortune (1891 – 1946) first alerted the world to the phenomenon of being psychically attacked in her best-selling book: 'Psychic Self-Defense', yet her words are as relevant today as they were in 1957 and, interestingly, the work continues to be regarded (deservedly so, in my opinion) as the definitive guide to detection and defense against psychic attack.

As a young woman Fortune, who was born into a family of Christian Scientists, worked as a law analyst at the Medico-Psychological Clinic in London. Her interest in exploring the human psyche led to her being psychically attacked. This occurred in 1911 when she was 29 years of age. Fortune worked in a school helping the principal who, for some unknown reason, took a vehement dislike to her. Unknown to Dion, this woman possessed a considerable knowledge of occultism obtained during a long residence in India. Although Fortune casts no aspersions on her attacker, it is more than evident from reading her account of the attack that principal was involved in the dark arts.

"It was her custom," Fortune wrote, "to control her staff by means of her knowledge of mind-power and she had a steady succession of the most peculiar breakdowns among the people working under her." (5)

When going to tell the woman that she was leaving her job, the principal subjected Fortune to vindictiveness, gazing deeply into her eyes, telling her that she lacked self-confidence and was utterly incompetent. Later on, Fortune admitted that this individual had conveyed the psychic attack through special yoga techniques and hypnotism all of which left her "a mental and physical wreck" for three years. As a result of her experience, Fortune came to the conclusion that hostile psychic energy can emanate both deliberately as well as unwittingly from certain people and that, if a victim is aware of these attacks and equipped to handle then they can be mentally successfully fended off.

Unfortunately, psychic attacks happen far more frequently than is supposed. Most people simply have no idea whatsoever of the sort of things that can be done by people who have knowledge of the powers of the human mind and of how the body's energy fields can be prey to such ill-intent.

Our energy field is a shimmering and dazzling shield of light, color and sound that exists in a world of similar energy. But, just as there is day, so too is there night. And the existence of earth-bound spirits, dark negative entities, demons, ghosts and energy vampires cannot be denied. Indeed some psychologists even estimate that more than 80% of people are in some way influenced by discarnate entities. The woman who suffers from multiple personality disorder is a prime example. It is sad, but true, that a lot of people who pass on and leave their bodies are not actually aware of the fact that they have undergone a 'transition' called death. In many ways, contemporary society with its focus on living provides us with little or no preparation for dealing with death. When a person has died in a car accident for instance, they may be aware that something has happened – but they may also feel very much alive in much the same way they did *before* the accident. The problem is that they don't have a physical body any more. If deceased relatives come to assist them to move forward, the dead person may actually run away from the dead body in the coffin! Such spirits may wander aimlessly around the world until they can either be released or else, find another physical body to 'possess'.

In a nutshell psychic attacks involve the manipulation and movement of different types of dark energies, entities and spirits. Some dark energies and entities that find their way into the physical and energetic bodies as well as the homes of victims are sent by other humans without conscious awareness. But, as an energy worker, I have to admit that there is little doubt that others are sent quite intentionally to create harm, often to control and manipulate and almost certainly to punish the individual in some way. Some attacks can be so powerful that they can render the unsuspecting victim a physical and nervous wreck indefinitely. The sending of these entities may involve the use of certain rituals or special ceremonies or rely simply on telepathy and hypnosis. Sometimes a combination of all of these factors is involved.

One of the prime methods used by these 'energy stealers' is known as *cording*.

Cords are energy bands extending from one being (a living

human, an earthbound spirit of a deceased human or a higher dimensional entity such as a demon) to a live person. Almost everyone has cords attached to them and whilst some of these 'links' are tremendously positive (such as the beautiful silver etheric cords between mother and child, for example), other cords can be potentially very damaging. In energy work, I often see sticky, black etheric ropes attached to an unsuspecting victim with the express purpose of achieving something quite specific – usually revenge or power over that person. One of the biggest tell tale signs is when a person feels as if "something is holding them back". That "something" is usually a cord.

Another method of attack is the use of 'objects'. I often see rusty nails, shards of glass, and knives in the back, ropes around the neck or even stakes of wood implanted in the spiritual bodies of some people. Once these have been cleared, the health of the affected person improves – often dramatically.

A wealthy middle-aged woman who had tried unsuccessfully for many years to have a child told me that after her last baby had been stillborn, she had gone to see a spiritual healer. This woman had given her a special spiritual 'key' that my client had accepted. When I made a diagnosis of the case, I saw a grey stone, the size of a large pebble embedded in the woman's heart, while in her uterus there were fragments of cut glass and razor blades. When I tuned into her aura, I sensed a dark presence at a distance. Following the trail, I came to a large Victorian house in north London and was led by my team of guides to one particular room where I saw the 'healer' busily engaged in performing a black magic ritual. On a table in the room, I saw a photograph of my client, which I removed. I then did some work on the patient, taking out the objects that had caused her so much pain and pouring white, then golden light into the affected organs. Although the woman afterwards expressed shock and surprise at what had happened to her, she admitted that she had been a regular 'patient' of this healer, whose fees had kept increasing...

Although it is tremendously difficult to penetrate an aura that is healthy and strong, auras can be weakened by negative emotions, through the regular use of drugs and alcohol or via smoking and, of course, through ill health.

Taking regular care of your spiritual body, your aura and chakras, *is as important as taking care of the health of your physical body.*

When you are forewarned, you are forearmed, as the saying goes and some psychic attacks can be quite easy to spot.

Have you ever been in the company of someone who quite literally "drains" you, leaving you feeling tired and *thirsty?* We probably all know of some "needy" person whose company we find a bit difficult. Not because they are necessarily unpleasant or because we simply cannot get on with them – but because they leave us feeling this way for no apparent reason. To make matters worse, these people may even say that they really, *really* enjoy being with us! Often, you may even quite like this person and are unable to understand why he/she leaves you feeling so tired and out of sorts. They sap your energy, asking continual questions, seeking ideas and opinions from others, which they then soak up, re-arrange and present as their own, while never really contributing anything new, different or original to whatever they are involved in. Then, once they have gathered this information, they move on. This person is what we call *an unconscious psychic vampire.*

The *intentional psychic vampire* however is clever, devious and manipulative. These attackers select a "target" that is vulnerable in some way (death in the family, house move, illness, upsetting career change, divorce etc.) Making themselves invaluable to their prey, they often attempt to portray themselves as a positive influence. They may even give photographs of themselves to their intended victims. I have known some give locks of their own hair, clothing or bits of paper with writing on them, even crystals or jewellery to the object of their attack! This type of attacker is almost always supremely arrogant and can get very angry if they sense any sort of resistance, as Dion Fortune found out when she attempted to quit her job. These vampires attack the psyche and can produce debilitating effects on the overall health and energy of the affected person. Falling into a profoundly deep sleep for 10-15 hours, as if drugged, is one such example.

Unfortunately, families can be prime platforms for this type of attack. Indeed, for the vampire, there are almost limitless opportunities: photographs taken at family gatherings, special food prepared for celebrations and the exchanging of presents – all can and frequently, are used by these predators.

We have all heard of the 'mother-in-law' from Hell, but in Anna's case, this was no joke. When Anna married Ernesto, his mother in Italy sent them a present: a statue of the Virgin Mary with the express instruction that Anna break off a small portion of the statue and eat it every day. At first, out of respect to her new husband, Anna did just this but soon started to feel unwell. She then hid the statue and promptly forgot about it. As the years went by however, nothing in the lives of either Anna or her family seemed to go right – to the extent, that when she called out for help, she was convinced (as was her husband) that they had been cursed. An inspection of the house and land showed no major energy imbalance, however my L-rods kept zoning in on a particular cupboard in the lounge room. When the contents of the cupboard were emptied, we found a small box inside of which was the statue wrapped in newspaper. When I held the figurine, an image of an elderly lady complete with prayer book and rosary beads came quite clearly into view. Anna recognized the description as that of her mother-in-law. I sensed that this woman did not want Anna to be her son's wife as she had taken him away to another country (Australia). The old lady was so angry with Anna that she had paid the local 'witch' to curse her. The statue was the result. By consuming tiny portions of the ornament, Anna would become barren, her health would deteriorate, rapidly and Ernesto would eventually return to his mother in Italy. I healed the statue, bringing it back into the white light of God and then explained to both Anna and Ernesto what had happened. Ernesto's mother had long since died, so together we sent compassion and forgiveness to her. As this was a relatively complex attack that had endured over many years, it was particularly lovely to see that neither wife nor husband harbored any ill will. This makes the entire healing process so much more rapid and the family's fortunes soon turned around.

Sometimes though dark spirits and entities can move into a physical body *by invitation.* This is a common experience of those who play around with ouija boards, for example. The human who is invaded in this way will betray a noticeable difference in character, taste and life-style. Often they take on the illnesses as well as the physical attributes of the spirit or entity occupying them to such an extent that there appears to be completely different personality change.

The other type of psychic attack that needs to be mentioned here is *negative thought forms.* A thought form is incredibly powerful and can have so much energy that it can actually crystallize and manifest as a subtle structure. When thought forms are pure and their motivation positive, an individual's energy field reverberates with the shining, white light of goodness. The person grows in spirituality. But when thought forms are negative, the opposite happens. The aura shrinks and chakras become clogged and slow down. Thought forms sent to others as a result of negative thinking, anger, jealously, animosity, vindictiveness, revenge, rage or fear can be lodged in a person's energy field or aura impacting adversely on the health and functioning of chakras and thereby wreaking all sorts of physical, emotional, mental and spiritual problems.

The degrees of strength of any of the attacks listed above can differ from low to medium to high. I must mention at this stage that it is important to understand that not all health or behavior problems are the result of a psychic attack and it is critical for healers to assess all factors.

We can also definitely draw these dark energies to ourselves and playing Harry Potter-like games with the occult is one such way to do this as is indulging in prolonged bouts of rage, anger or resentment. Bitterness will make you bitter. Violence of all kinds is another very powerful draw for negative/dark energy.

Mary's case is fairly typical. The youngest of three siblings, as the years went by she became progressively resentful of her more successful sisters. They were attractive, intelligent and happily married with children. Mary, on the other hand, was pretty much a loner. As a teenager, her curiosity had led to her dabbling in drugs and witchcraft. With the breakdown of her marriage, she had moved closer to her aging parents to "keep an eye on them". But, as time marched on, she became increasingly bitter with her lot in life and drank and smoked fairly heavily. With the death of her father from a sudden cancer, she gradually took control of her mother's affairs and eventually became her sole beneficiary. At the old lady's funeral a few years later, her sisters remarked that they "should hardly have known" Mary – the alteration in her physical appearance being so pronounced. After the service, Mary gave her sisters special books that bore her signature as a remembrance of the funeral. Within two years, both sisters had died of cancer.

Mary's story is a prime example of malicious and deliberate psychic attack. It is highly likely that she had been taken over by a discarnate entity through her youthful adventures into the dark side of the occult and I found it interesting to note that her appearance had also altered significantly. She had gained a great deal of weight, was very bitter at her lot in life and had actually come to look like a different person. Drinking, smoking and drug taking would have weakened her aura considerably, enabling the entity to penetrate her fairly easily and even more deeply. She was really quite defenseless. I also found it interesting that the deceased family members suffered from cancer – a disease that wields a disturbing and pronounced effect on the body's energy matrix where, in my opinion, it is born.

Today, many books are published giving the average person access to spells, incantations and magical potions for negative energies. I would like to emphasize that there is enormous power in these spells. They can create havoc and harm when used to control, manipulate or punish others *in any way and will always return to the sender inflicting much damage and paving the way for access by demonic entities.*

If you suspect that you are a victim of this type of attack, please seek help from an experienced energy worker of good intent to help clear all of these attachments.

ANGELS FOR GOD

Yet, in spite of the ever-present menace of psychic attacks, whenever our physical energy is at low ebb, there is always the comforting presence of *Angels.*

These celestial beings of light, so vibrant with energy, have protected and guarded human kind since before the dawn of time. They remain the ultimate source of energetic power on the earth.

They are also the supreme form of subtle energy for they are divine and they touch our transitory lives in a multitude of amazing and often karmic ways. They are our connection with God because they are the bridge between our two worlds. They are the essence of love and joy and stem from the heart of God with whom they enjoy an intimate relationship. They flock around the universe in their millions, as numerous as the stars in the heavens and they are dedicated to serve the needs of free will entities (humans) so that we may experience the same level of unconditional love as they do. *Everyone has Angels around them constantly and without exception and they are eager and excited about the opportunity to communicate with you.*

Whenever my life has been touched by the presence of Angels, I see tall, glowing beings with no wings, whose eyes hold the energy of God. I am always filled with amazement and wonderment. At such moments I have no awareness of time at all – for time seems to stand completely still.

Although most people may not be able to see the Guardian Angels allotted to them at birth, angels have always been by the side of mankind. They closed the earthly paradise, protected Lot, saved Hagar and her child, stayed Abraham's hand, communicated the law, led the People of God to the Promised Land, announced births and callings, assisted the prophets and proclaimed the coming of Christ. They are also catalysts for Armageddon – the final battle with the forces of darkness....As humans, we are simply surrounded by the loving adoration and the service of angels.

The word 'angel' is thought to be derived from the Greek word *Angelos,* which means 'messenger'. In Christian, Muslim, Jewish and other theologies an angel can be one who acts as a messenger, attendant or agent of God. According to the Jewish mystical work, *The Zohar,* angels came into being the moment God said: "let there be light; and there was light". They were created on the first day of Creation to have a continuous and permanent existence on the side of goodness and they are said to shine as brightly today, as they did on that very first day.

Angels are spirits without bodies who possess superior intelligence, incredible strength and surpassing holiness. They were created with one purpose – to love and serve all without condition, to affirm the reality of God as awareness and to expand His Spiritual Light. Angels hold the focus of pure love throughout the universe and are able to *set up a resonance for the vibration of pure love whenever it is needed.*

We, on the other hand, are free will entities. This means that we have chosen to develop our ability to exist with unconditional love by gaining much experience through many lifetimes (reincarnation) and many varied forms of existence. Angels have been created to counterbalance any energies or actions that move in the opposite direction to love so that we will eventually remember our true essence and attain the state of *Nirvana* – the path that leads to the cessation of suffering and the dissolving of desire, hatred and illusion.

For all our skepticism and "healthy scientific minds", we remain fascinated by angels. There have been numerous television shows such as 'Touched by an Angel', which screened for an incredible 10 years and was watched by millions of people around the world. And who doesn't remember the touchingly beautiful Frank Capra film 'It's a Wonderful Life', where the disillusioned hero James Stewart is saved from committing suicide by the timely intervention of his lovely, meek Guardian Angel, the aptly named Clarence Oddbody ('Every time a bell rings, an angel gets a pair of wings')?

Angels are a reminder not only of the fragility of the physical body, but of the inherent joy of the spiritual existence. They give us hope for a brighter, better future, they help us to attain Nirvana, for they alone represent the fundamental nature of Prana, which is, quite simply, goodness.

CONCLUSION

When controversial British novelist D.H. Lawrence (1885 – 1930) was about to embark on his great 'savage pilgrimage', he wrote: "Different places on the face of the earth have different vital effluence, different vibration, different chemical exhalation, different polarity with different stars; call it what you like, *but the spirit of place is a great reality"*.

The First World War had ended and Lawrence together with his wife, Frieda, was eager to turn his back on Western civilization in a bid to seek a more fulfilling life than that offered by industrial society. In the light of contemporary journeys into the ever-evolving dynamics of the Mind-Body-Spirit paradigm,

Lawrence's words were truly prophetic.

As humans, from the moment of conception, we are swathed in energy patterns of one kind or another. Throughout our lives we remain exquisitely sensitive to this energy matrix. However we quantify it (as Prana or Chi or opt to observe its workings in the more mechanical equations of mathematics and physics), this energy pulses endlessly throughout the universe. However it has only been in the last few years with the dawning of the so called 'Spirituality Revolution' that we, in the West, have stopped to consider the impact this energy has had on our existence and that of our planet.

With the transformation of orthodox religion and the incredible surge of interest in all things spiritual, we have come to develop not only a more responsible 'planetary consciousness' but, strange to say, we have found ourselves moving closer to God. Unfortunately, it has to be said that we are also in the midst of a resurgence in deep black magic and the arts of witchcraft, much of which currently masquerades as white magic, The popularity of this dubious movement, with its crystal-wearing, mandala-worshipping and earth-loving initiates, is highly disturbing and can only be likened to the Middle Ages when alchemy, secret societies and the dark arts flourished. The 'New Age' movement with its worship of the 'gods', where man becomes a 'god' and where channellers receive messages from 'Lord Maitreya' is nothing less than demonism. Egyptian paganism and Masonic philosophies are now everywhere, as are psychics who claim to converse with the dead. Beware the so-called 'healers' who look deeply into your aura and start talking about your 'past lives'!

It is critical to remember that whatever we decide to talk about – be it magic, spirituality, reincarnation, parapsychology, environmentalism or even futurism, what we are essentially talking or writing about or even listening to is *energy*.

When you are tuned into this zone, I can promise you that

nothing in your life will ever be the same. This is a warning as well as a statement.

Universal Prana is not bound in time or space – it exists around us. It is profoundly sensitive to our needs and flows from every living thing to all things.

We are essentially spiritual pilgrims who choose to walk a human path. Together, let us embark on this journey towards greater health and happiness. Let us now take a look at some of the 70,000 veils that surround God, the greatest cosmic vibrating force there is and the essence of all life in the universe, as we know it

"The Breeze at dawn has secrets to tell you.
Don't go back to sleep.
You must ask for what you really want.
Don't go back to sleep.
People are going back and forth across the doorsill
Where the two worlds touch.
The door is round and open.
Don't go back to sleep."
RUMI (1207 – 1273)

References:

(1) "Move to a new Planet", says Hawking." BBC News, November 30, 2006.

(2) Emoto, M. 'The Hidden Messages in Water', Beyond Words Publishing Inc. USA. 2004.

(3) Shumsky, S. 'Exploring Auras'. Foreword by Dannion Brinkley. New Page Books. USA. 2006.

(4 Leviton, R. 'The Galaxy on Earth: A Traveler's Guide to the Planet's Visionary Geography'. Hampton Roads Pub. Co. USA. 2002.

(5) Fortune, D. 'Psychic Self-Defense'. Aquarian/Thorsons. UK. 1988.

PART TWO:

ANGELS AND DEMONS
– THE BREEZE AT DAWN

DEATH & THE BIRTH OF PRANA

"Everyone dies, but no-one is dead."
TIBETAN SAYING

Any exploration into the dynamics of the human energy field must start with death.

Christians say: "In my end, is my beginning", while Buddhists believe passionately that it is only through the process of dying and eventual death that we truly learn about life. Transmigration of the soul also plays an important part in Hinduism, Jainism, Sikhism and other Indian religions. In the final moments of mortal life we are said to hold, within us, the tension of the paradox of our life, the spark of a new life, the workings of a new consciousness, even of a new fate. The great cycle of Prana actually begins here.

Knowledge of the mysteries of death is therefore a major key to unlocking the Pranic code of universal energy.

Sadly the last fifty years have witnessed a decline in teachings on death in Western nations. For peoples of the First World the emphasis is very much on *living*, on getting as much out of life while you can and, in some instances, of even *defying* death. Today, an entire industry has sprung up fuelled by many people's desire to stay forever young. For millions of westerners old age and death are simply not accepted as a natural part of life anymore. Lulled by the false comforts of medical and technological advancement, western culture continues to dream that 'progress' will somehow 'domesticate' once and for all the senseless malignancy of death. *But death is the one inevitability for every living thing on the planet. Death comes to us all.* There is nothing we can do to stop it however hard we try. And, when it does come, we tend to expect an automatic, painless oblivion. A journey into nothingness. For millions of westerners, the contemporary God-less perspective on death is almost anaesthetic.

In the East however, death is seen as a door through which we must pass on a transition that can be worse than fatally dangerous for the unprepared or badly misdirected soul.

The Tibetan people take death so seriously that their lamas have written guidebooks for the journey between past, present and future lives. The *'Tibetan Book of the Dead'* (or *'Bardo Thodol'*) is popularly known in the West as *'The Great Book of Natural Liberation through understanding in the Between'*.

In Tibet, the last great frontier of raw spirituality on earth, the local people are more concerned about the spiritual conquest of the inner universe (death, the 'between' states of existence and rebirth) than any other race I have met.

The Dalai Lamas and several thousand "reincarnate" Lamas are believed to have mastered the 'death/rebirth cycle' and to choose continuously, life after life, to return to Tibet out of compassion to lead the Tibetans in their spiritual lives and to help all sentient beings. The present reincarnation of the living Buddha, the Dalai Lama often quips that he cannot die, that he is destined to remain with the human race until Nirvana is at last attained.

The teachings of the New Testament clearly state that Christ will be "with us…until the end of time", while the annual Lenten passage is focused very much on growing through death. The power of the crucifixion for all Christians lies in the resurrection of the Son of Man – through His death, the human race has been liberated. This and this alone is the enduring power of the cross over the darkness of night.

As prana flowed out of the physical body of Jesus, the light of the sun was eclipsed in one of the most powerful and moving passages of New Testament script. Indeed the Easter Triduum resonates with this 'between' energy – of how such energy was dimmed at the moment of Christ's death and of how it was restored in all its brilliancy at His resurrection.

The parallels between these two great spiritual disciplines (Buddhism and Christianity) on the critical subject matter of mortality simply cannot be ignored and while eastern teachings on death are the most widely known – they are by no means unique. What really surprised me during the course of my research was the fact that these ancient books of the dead have their counterparts in our own western cultural traditions, traditions that have long since been forgotten.

In the twilight years of the Middle Ages a guidebook on death called the *'Ars Morendi'* or *'The Art of Dying'* was in widespread use throughout Austria, Germany, France and Italy. The focus of the work was two-fold: to elaborate on the experience of dying and to provide concrete instructions for the dying person and their helpers during the last hours of mortal life. Essential to "a good death" was said to be a courageous confrontation of death – avoidance of death and a reluctance to surrender to it were considered to be two of the major dangers facing the dying individual.

How then do you define death?

According to the Oxford English Dictionary death is the "final cessation of vital functions" (1). From the perspective of western medicine, it is the cessation of heartbeat and brain activity – the "flatline" on the EEG. Death is the ultimate scientific concept of nothingness. It is the "I" that ceases to be and the void that swallows up life.

Feared by the contented, and dismissed by the rich, death can also be welcomed by individuals who live in perpetual misery or by those who grapple day after day with unbearable pain or anguish. Gravestones down through the centuries bear testimony to this latter attitude and have likened death to a state of deep sleep filled with peace, ever-lasting rest and perpetual silence.

But, from an energy viewpoint, death is far from being a "nothing" and it seems so strange to me that we liken death to an activity that we are all seemingly so fond of. Whilst we love our beds, sleep does not equate with a flatline and bears no resemblance whatsoever to a total lack of brain activity. Scientifically speaking, we know that our sleep is positively crammed with activity – often more so than during our waking hours! The sleep state is completely different from the death state of a corpse. Yet the universal fear of death persists.

Why?

The truth is that we are afraid of death *not because we know it is nothing, but because we know instinctively that it cannot bring us nothing.*

And, as usual, our instinct is right.

As the death process occurs, prana is cut off from its thread-like connection at the navel and is freed from the shell of the physical body. The subtle body, which remains unchanged and which holds within it all the elements for a new life, then leaves the physical through one of the special gates that are linked to the *Nadis* network.

The visible manifestation of the exit of prana for all humans is bleeding/weeping eyes or nose, or open mouth or nose. The last 'gasp' of life or the 'death throes', as it is sometimes poetically referred to, is prana leaving the confines of the body. As the great Victorian novelist Charles Dickens (1812-1870) lay dying, those sitting at his bedside noticed that a large tear welled up from his right eye and trickled down his cheek as he breathed his last. Thus prana left his body.

Many religious teachings insist that if we accept death as part of life, then when death does come, we will accept it more easily. And this acceptance is critical to the journey that the spiritual body, or soul, is now set to undertake. For if we do not come to understand what lies between death and rebirth while we are alive, prana can get sucked into a spiral of anxiety and uncertainty as death beckons. Overcoming this state is critical for the soul cannot enter a new body or ascend to another dimension without its pranic 'lifeblood'.

With the death of the body, the soul does not evaporate into nothingness, but instead embarks on a great spiritual journey.

The connection between these limitless dimensions and universes is *karma,* the universal law of cause and effect.

In fact life between birth and death is a veritable field of karma in which we sow, reap and sow again. Our physical body may wither, but our karma, so the saying goes, lives on.

While we mutate through different life forms from life to life, our karma remains the subtle force that shapes our incarnations with every decision we ever make. Good deeds lead to rebirth in a higher state. Evil deeds may lead to rebirth as a slave or even as an animal.

Karma has been likened to the lighting of one candle from another – is the light of the second the same as the first? The simile is truly beautiful when understood. Light one candle from another and the light is the same, *yet different.* This is karma.

Today, the twin concepts of *karma* and *reincarnation* are used time and again by people to explain their actions, to answer questions of universal poverty, despair, even great wealth. There is little doubt that these states seem to offer the most attractive explanations for mankind's origin and destiny. A recent US survey has revealed that a quarter of all Americans believe in some form of reincarnation. I find this intriguing because it states acceptance of a spiritual dimension – not just by adherents of Eastern religions such as Buddhism and Hinduism – but by those who do not share such religious or esoteric beliefs.

To know that you have lived possibly many lives before this one and that there may be more lifetimes in the wings, can be a source of great comfort for those seeking to be liberated from their current situation – whatever that situation may be.

In many ways, karma and reincarnation go hand in hand for they tell us that our soul, as it journeys along the patterns of birth, maturation and death has the renewed opportunity of rebirth and with it, the renewed opportunity to grow in goodness, to expand in love, to overcome the trials and tribulations of this lifetime. Karma and reincarnation remind us that everything we do today, we have been building towards for many, many years...

Energy is indestructible, because God, the ultimate source of all energy, is indestructible. But energy can be altered and can be transformed at many levels.

As the soul is liberated from the body, the transition to a new rebirth is seen as the best time to dissolve negative karma and to alter energetic flow.

Interestingly, the time and place of death is always known beforehand by the Spiritual Hierarchy as well as by the inner realms of the individual's soul.

The many thousands of documented NDEs provide us with a fairly clear picture of what to expect during the process of death and these experiences correspond with the *bardos,* or three main stages of death, as contained in the *Book of Natural Liberation.*

All of these NDEs are consistent on certain fundamentals: they describe a feeling of being separated from the body, of floating gently above it before passing through a tunnel with enormous bright lights at the end of it. Survivors speak of coming into the presence of this extraordinary light, of being surrounded by luminous beings in a world awash with dazzling colors and hues, amid scenes of intense beauty. The perfume of flowers is said to be exquisite, while the colors of nature are quite simply overwhelming. Others report a moving recollection of their entire life pass before them.

These recollections are not the ravings of the deluded. According to ancient records, they speak the truth.

The *Book of Liberation,* for example, is recited by lamas over a dying or recently deceased person, or sometimes even over and effigy of the deceased to guide the subtle energetic body through the major realms of: *chikha* (the bardo of the moment of death), *chonyid* (the bardo of the experience of reality) and *sidpa* (the bardo of rebirth). The Dalai Lama has written that the final phase in the process of dying actually happens when the experience of the "clear light of reality", or the nearest approximation to it of which one is spiritually capable, occurs. Until this time, Buddhists believe that the dead person can still hear and is acutely conscious of what is happening around them. If there is much mourning and sadness around the dead person during this period, it can cause great confusion for the soon to be departed soul.

It is during this all-important time that a highly trained practitioner will attempt to move the deceased towards a greater realization of ultimate truth and of the emptiness of physical existence through prayers and meditations. In the final stages of death, the "mother clear light", which dawns at death due to karma, is transformed into a spiritual path consciousness.

The texts guide the soul (now feeling lighter in the absence of the heavy gravitational pull of the earth) on its often perilous journeys through hells, the realms of hungry ghosts or Pretans, which are incarnations of hunger, thirst, craving and frustration. All the while, the priest advises the subtle body to choose carefully, steering it though the eight signs of death – the maze of mirage, smoke, fireflies, the flame of a butter lamp, the dawning of vivid colors (white, red-orange and blackness) before the unfolding of the 'child clear' light and the stirring of a new cycle of energy.

The texts also remind us that it is incredibly fortuitous to be reborn as a human. For only humans are given the opportunity to consciously create karmas. Through karma we are impelled to float along the river of life. Along this journey we meet other souls also impelled by karma. We may become attached to one another, spend time together and then part. We may even try to linger, but as ever karma carries us on. The traveler does not always experience a pleasant trip though – due to our earthly attachments we can experience many things: pleasure, pain, loss, gain, joy, suffering and so on. We can get caught in karmic whirlpools and despite the cycle of death and rebirth, still end up getting spiritually nowhere. Then, *instead of being the creator of our karmas, we are created by them.*

Freedom from the bondage of karma allows the individual to grow, to evolve. Only those highly evolved adepts who are free from karma can leave their body consciously before death draws near.

At death, the astral body becomes refined, as the physical body falls away.

As the death process is completed, the new soul is given access in the spirit world to the Akashic Records – the universal database of all events that have ever occurred, as well as every thought and action of every individual.

Having reviewed our former lives, we are now given an opportunity to alter our future karmas.

Unless karma requires an immediate return to earth (as in the case of a life interrupted by suicide, for example), most subtle bodies will spend some time residing on the Spiritual level helping to serve others who have recently 'crossed over' or by passing down spiritual strength and guidance to loved ones back on earth.

Some yogis and other spiritual masters have the ability through powerful concentration techniques to generate a special energy called *Tumo* which moves upwards from the solar plexus chakra point to the top of the head (the crown chakra), before moving back down into the lower body via the throat, heart and navel chakras as well as the sexual organs, allowing special energy vibrations known as 'joys' (joy, supreme joy, special joy and innate joy) to manifest. These vibrations make it possible to transform a spiritual path consciousness at the precise moment of death. Yogis are said to leave the physical body through the top of the skull, the gateway along which *kundalini*, powerful pranic energy, passes.

All human babies are born with the kundalini portal open. We call this sacred gate the 'soft spot' and kundalini flows freely throughout the meridian and chakra pathways before the gap closes at approximately six months of age – effectively severing links with the spiritual realms.

Kundalini is derived from the Sanskrit word *'Kundal'* meaning 'coiled up' as this primordial dominant energy is quite literally coiled up, like a serpent, at the base of the spine, known as the Sacrum or tailbone. The closest equivalent we in the West have to this extraordinary energy is the Christian concept of the Holy Ghost, the energy of God in the universe.

Kundalini is said to nourish the tree of life in all humans and has been revered down through the ages as a seat of great power. As we grow in spirituality, Kundalini is awakened, rising up from the base of the spine, opening up the chakras and endowing the body with extraordinary health, energy and, of course, enlightenment. It has been said that a full kundalini awakening activates all past karma immediately leading to a profound restructuring of mind, body and spirit.

In Latin, this part of the body is called 'Os Sacrum' suggesting that it is a holy or sacred area. The ancient Greeks called this bone the 'Hieron Osteon', noting that it was the last bone to be destroyed when the body was burnt. The Egyptians too considered it to be a seat of special power, while in the West, Sacrum is symbolized by the sign of Aquarius and the Holy Grail, container of the water of life itself.

A good life and a good death – our evolution as a species reverberates with images of death. The ancient Celts, for example, amazed their Roman overlords by their complete fearlessness of death and their staunch belief in reincarnation. The Greek writer Diordus Siculus (c.60BC-39AD) recorded that the Celtic priesthood, the Druids, believed that: "The souls of men are immortal and that after a definite number of years, they (the Celts) live a second life when the soul passes to another body". Even Julius Caesar wrote of the Celts: "They wish to inculcate this as one of their leading tenets, that souls do not become extinct, but pass after death from one body to another, and they think that men by this tenet are in a great degree stimulated to valor, the fear of death being disregarded."

The native North American Red Indian aspired to the Happy Hunting Ground, while Viking warriors were transported by the Valkyries, the fierce battle-maidens of Odin, the Norse god of war and death, to Valhalla – hall of the slain. There is the Isle of Avalon, where King Arthur still sleeps and, of course, the ultimate goal for many remains the pearly gates of Heaven, presided over by none other a personage than St. Peter, complete with celestial keys.

Kabbalistic writings, in particular the Zohar, give some of the most beautiful and moving explanations of soul transmigration I have ever read.

In this text, two guardian angels are said to guide the soul into the mortal realms, depositing the embryo into the future mother's womb, while setting a light over the soul so that it can see throughout the Worlds. As the soul is given information on the Laws of Creation, it realizes the rewards and possibilities for a life lived in a state of higher bliss, or a lower one lived in misery. With free choice and a brief on what task it is to perform in the World, the soul is then shown a model plan of its life to be lived, the people it will encounter on this journey and the places it will pass through. Acutely aware that its presence is to realize the presence of God in this particular time and place within the physical universe, the soul is then left in the womb for nine months with this knowledge, until birth, when this information is closed off and the soul sets out on its journey in the world....

The Old Testament provides a valuable source of examples of karmic law with penalties being extracted for harmful or devious actions. The death of the child Bathsheba bore to King David being seen as atonement for David's sin (by coveting another man's wife) when he sent Bathsheba's husband, Uriah the Hittite up to the front-lines in battle, where he was killed. Christ Himself talked openly about reincarnation with His Sermon on the Mount being a perfect example of karmic law. Here Jesus taught: "Judge not, lest you be judged…Blessed are the merciful, for they shall obtain mercy". Later, at His capture by Temple Guards in the garden at Gethsemane, Jesus rebuked the apostle Peter to put his sword away: "He who lives by the sword dies by the sword". Early Church Father, Saint Gregory, the Bishop of Nyssa, noted: "It is absolutely necessary that the soul shall be healed and purified, and if it does not take place in one life on earth, it must be accomplished in future earthly lives."

Later on, in 533AD reincarnation was declared a heresy by the Council of Constantinople, with the declaration that mortal man has but one life in which to merit eternal reward or damnation. Despite this ruling, many Christians (lay as well as clergy) continue to believe in reincarnation to this day.

SPIRIT RELEASEMENT

"I have not slept for three hundred years," he said sadly, and Virginia's beautiful blue eyes opened in wonder; "for three hundred years I have not slept, and I am so tired."
'THE CANTERVILLE GHOST' by Oscar Wilde.

Unfortunately, those who do not believe in the realm of the Spirit or whose attachment to earthly life is pronounced can get a little 'stuck' when death takes place.

Not everyone dies slowly, for example.

In a sudden accident, there may not be time to notice the signs of death or, as in the case of Sir Simon de Canterville, sometimes a deceased person can remain earthbound due to a particular problem such as anger, hatred or revenge or even a physical addiction.

One rather simple way of explaining ghosts is that they are spiritual implants in an environment during a period of intense emotional activity. I am acutely conscious of electro-magnetic 'impressions' left in this way after a murder, a battle or some other terrible accident has occurred in the place where I am dowsing. Sometimes this energy can actually be heard, seen or physically felt. My hands often vibrate painfully as if I have had an electric shock when I am in the midst of such 'stuck energy'or I will experience an unpleasant taste in my mouth as of dry blood, for example.

One of the most significant examples of this is, of course, the Tower of London. As a teenager on school trips to this historic site, there were some areas I distinctly recall feeling very uncomfortable in though I had no idea why this should have been so at the time. I was especially disturbed by The Bloody Tower and the Martin Tower as well as the Green. Later on, I found out why.

For literally thousands of years, the Tower has soaked up the sight and sound of torture, murder, execution, suicide and almost every conceivable kind of human misery.

There have been scores of well-attested sightings throughout the network of buildings that comprise the famous city landmark. The ghost of Anne Boleyn, second wife of Henry VIII and mother of Elizabeth I, has often been seen in an upper room of the Martin Tower where she was held prisoner before her execution. Yeoman Warder Geoffrey Abbot once told the famous physic investigator Peter Underwood of several instances when night patrols had heard screams through the heavy doors of the White Tower leading to the torture chambers.

But ghosts at the Tower can also appear initially as normal flesh-and-blood people. In 1970, a tourist visiting the Bloody Tower observed a woman with long hair standing by a window. She wore an ankle-length black velvet dress, a white cap and a large gold medallion around her neck. As the visitor was thinking that it was someone wearing period costume, the 'woman' began to fade before her eyes and finally completely disappeared. Intrigued, the tourist returned a few weeks later and was astonished to observe the same phenomenon again and in exactly the same place.

What is going on?

When human beings avoid the white light of pure energy because of addictions such as alcohol, drugs, sex or intense fear their energies can become bogged down during the dying process. *These attachments to earthly life lock the subtle body into an earthbound existence, until it can be released.*

A person who liked to drink, for example, upon dying, may rush to the nearest bar. The problem is, of course, that now the individual does not have a physical body and consequently the only way to satisfy the craving for alcohol is by possessing someone else's body, which he promptly does. Sometimes, the possessing person can be so upset with the individual who wronged him that he simply refuses to ascend to the spiritual plane until he gets the opportunity to wreak revenge.

Hospitals, graveyards, funeral homes and battlefields are some of the more common environments where such problems occur – anywhere, in short, where a lot of people die or are likely to congregate due to certain cravings or addictions (bars, drug parties etc.). During the 1800s in Australia, pubs were the preferred place of repose before burial. At one of Melbourne's first public houses The Lamb Inn, a bushranger's body with a bullet in his forehead, lay on the billiard table for several days in 1842 before it could be interred. It is hardly surprising therefore to find that to this day, many Australian pubs are hotspots for paranormal sightings and psychic contamination.

Sometimes, a fragment of the deceased person's energy may even possess an individual during organ transplants. Some heart transplant recipients have subsequently reported actually feeling the energy of their late donors much to the confusion and consternation of their health care providers! Examples include an

American lady with vertigo who became a climber and a 7 year-old who had nightmares about being killed after being given the heart of a murdered child.

In the recently screened ABC television documentary: 'Thanks for the Memories' (2) patients in the US and Britain talked openly about the changes to their lives, their food preferences and their abilities in the wake of organ transplants. Claire Brennan, the first successful heart and lung transplant patient in New England, remarked on her changing eating habits – chicken nuggets, beer and green peppers – and of a dream in which she was told (quite correctly as it later turned out) of her donor's name: Timothy. Claire later came to feel powerfully that she was living with the presence of another person inside of her.

Other patients meanwhile attested to a range of startling post-operative changes – a gush of creative writing (in the case of a modestly educated middle-aged married man), a sudden unexplained passion for classical music in another instance and an insatiable urge for body-building in one previously desk-bound executive who later discovered that he had been given the heart of a Hollywood stunt man!

The panel of medical and scientific experts interviewed offered a range of interesting possibilities as to why these changes could be occurring. These included the fact that the heart is intimately connected to the brain via neural pathways, as well as the technically impressive fact that the heart radiates a powerful magnetic energy field.

From the scientific point of view, such analyses are eminently feasible and are called "cellular memory phenomenon". But from the perspective of energy healing, these hypotheses are only partly correct.

The simple truth is that each and every organ in the physical body vibrates with prana and every cell in the human body carries the characteristics of that soul's body.

It is this unique, individual energy that the recipients are feeling so powerfully as their physical and subtle bodies align to accommodate the energy of the deceased person.

In the case of heart recipients, for example, *the body of the patient now beats to the heart chakra of another's prana.* As far as energy workers are concerned, the spiritual and physical bodies retain past memories – right down to the cellular level. Nothing is erased.

In the vast majority of cases, I have no doubt that such energy exchange operates on the most positive of levels.

The gift of life that one human being gives to another is profoundly special and is not taken up without a great deal of contemplation and compassion.

But, there are instances, during which organs have been taken without permission (such as in the case of prisoners who have been systematically executed for example) when problems can occur.

In these cases, there may be much anger or resentment on the part of the deceased at having their lives taken so suddenly from them. This low energy will reside in their physical bodies and may well be felt later on by the unsuspecting donor. When the donor begins to feel this anger or fear etc. he/she may well end up feeding this energy without realizing it. By doing so, the negative pattern of emotion will be encouraged. Sometimes the donor may have no idea of what is wrong or even different, friends may make remarks about the dramatic personality changes or the mood swings they witness but the donor can fail to recognize these alterations.

It is now that spirit releasement techniques must come into their own. This vital process entails helping both human and non-human entities to experience the Light of pure white energy – even by becoming aware that this Light of God is already within them.

Unfortunately, some humans and non-human entities seem to prefer to avoid the bright white Light that appears as the body is about to separate from the mind at death - either because they have been taught to fear it or because they are busy denying its existence. These beings may also have feelings of unworthiness. Dark entities, for example, believe fervently that the Light will melt them and cause them to cease to exist. The darker the entity, the greater the fear.

During spirit releasement, professional healers often call upon the aid of the Archangel Michael to restrain the dark entity until it is willing to listen. This is not an easy task as some dark forces often lash out kicking and screaming at the very thought of moving on.

In the presence of angelic light, negative barriers can be gently lifted thus enabling the earthbound spirit to listen to its true feelings and be guided towards the positive, loving Light of God.

In the Book of Revelation, the seven Archangels who stand before God carry Divine Decrees to connect intimately with us on earth. Michael - whose name is a question: "Who is like God?" – remains one of the greatest of all angels. He is the angel of the Sabbath Day, is God's Champion, the patron of Israel and Prince of Light. It is Michael who subdued Satan, the Prince of Evil, and who banished him from Heaven in single combat.

Visionaries down through the centuries have revealed that Michael wears a cloak of cobalt blue and carries an unsheathed sword of living flame, which can cut through the cords that bind us to negative emotions and past lives. It is this cord cutting that is used in releasement.

Healers will often ask St. Michael to throw a net of Light over the entity or unhappy spirit and to slowly draw it tighter until the spirit is willing to listen. Some will request that the entity be encapsulated in a beacon of Light. Almost without exception, spirit releasement specialists will ask St. Michael to direct a shaft of light through the net to show that the Light cannot harm, melt or destroy the entity in any way.

The trapped spirit is then instructed to look deep within him/her and report what he/she can see. Most of them immediately say that they can see a tiny white light. At this stage no suggestion is offered about the true nature of the Light – the dark entity or unhappy spirit is just asked to continue focusing on the spark of Light. Without exception, all of the trapped spirits will report that the Light is growing bigger and bigger, brighter and more dazzling than before. The healer continues to urge the spirit to keep looking at the Light until, gradually, there is nothing but the Light. All of the darkness has simply gone. Often the darker the entity, the more they will plead to bask in the Light before they call other dark beings to also see the Light in the darkness.

For unsuspecting humans who are stuck, the process of releasement is a little different. Many healers often call upon relatives, friends and lovers of the deceased who have successfully crossed over into the spirit realm to come and help them move the spirit soul to the Light, replacing feelings of anger and fear with those of joy and peace.

There are some dark entities, of course, that are simply not destined to move towards the light. Their end is total darkness – the inevitability of energy forms that have not progressed through their respective incarnations. And, while the majority of NDE cases reported tend to be positive ones where the person is left with an overwhelming feeling of being totally loved by God, there are recorded instances of nightmarish encounters in the realms of Hell.

Those few individuals who have spoken openly about this traumatic experience have had their lives transformed too – but from the opposite end of the spectrum, so to speak. When I hear such men and women speak, I am always touched by their candidness, their sincerity and above all, by their humility. All of these NDE recipients have been given a second chance – and each and every one of these remarkable opportunities has the power to transform.

Throughout many of his teachings on death and reincarnation, His Holiness the Dalai Lama advises that in the event of sudden death, it is important to try to focus on the quality of compassion, to remember that everything is pure and not to dwell on anger, hatred, ego or earthly attachments. "Father, forgive them, they know not what they do" – this was the first of the last seven statements that Christ made as he lay dying in exquisite agony on the Cross. They reveal as nothing else does, that the Son of Man was filled with a deep compassion towards his enemies, that he was completely freed from hatred. As He moved towards the golden Light of divinity, Jesus conquered the shadow of death to liberate the soul of mankind...

Through the intangible cycle of rebirth, we learn that we are made in the image of God and that we exist in an infinite field of unfolding possibility. Above all, we learn that we *are* energy.

CHAKRAS AND AURIC BODIES – THE WORLD WITHIN & THE WORLD WITHOUT

"Do you imagine that we see the hundred thousandth part of what exists?
Consider, for example, the wind. The wind whistles, groans, bellows, sometimes even kills. Have you seen it?"
Guy de Maupassant (1850-1893)

Thus reincarnation ignites the flame that, in turn, sparks the creation of the human energy matrix.

Encoded into this matrix is the *Chakra System* and other interlinking networks along which and through which the divine essence of Prana now surges. As a new human body is created, it is swathed in the manifold sheaths of subtle energy fields or *auras*. Dazzlingly brilliant rainbow-like hues visible to psychics and other enlightened beings, these sheaths pulsate around the physical body in what I refer to as 'The Dance of Life'.

Inside the body, meanwhile, another 'dance' is in progress also interacting with the invisible energy of the universe. Moving freely into and through auric fields and around the physical body via the meridian conduits, chakras are our storehouses and transmitters of Prana as it courses through them in spiral-like movements. The Chakra system is our interface with the universal life force, as it works in acutely subtle ways to sustain life itself.

Invisible to the naked eye, the chakras have been described in ancient eastern texts as wheels in motion, specific in color and lying directly along the spine in a rod-like formation starting from the base of the spine (Root Chakra) and ending at the top of the cranium (Crown chakra). They are said to measure less than $1/8^{th}$ of an inch in diameter and to rotate at a specific speed in direct alignment with the frequency of the information to which they are so intimately tuned. The sheer vitality of each flattened, funnel-shaped chakra is said to be a determining factor in the deterioration or vitality of the human body. Interestingly, each chakra color is identical to the colors of the rainbow. Physics describes the electromagnetic spectrum as a narrow band of radiant information just above "Infrared" and just below "Ultraviolet". The Chakra System displays an identical light spectrum, as we shall see. The Root Chakra, for example, is red and resonates to vibrations occurring in this 'red frequency range' thus impacting on the health of the endocrine gland to which it is intimately connected – in this case the gonads.

In aging or illness, the chakras collapse into the physical body and slow their rate of rotation. An ancient Tibetan prescription for restoring wellbeing of both mind and body involves a series of movements or "rites" designed to maintain the vitality and spin-rate of the Chakras. Recommended as a daily meditation, these once secret movements are not aerobic in nature and are used in monasteries throughout Tibet as a mode of prayer and meditation as well as physical maintenance.

Just as the physical body needs a regular intake of food to energize the organs and muscles, the subtle body too needs a regular uptake of 'soul food' or prana to keep it balanced and in harmony with the universe.

We have been conditioned to assume that if everything is working out well for us in the physical world that we will be content with our life. But this is simply not the case.

Today money might remain the currency of a successful life, but we are increasingly living in a world where real wealth is being measured not by dollars, but by personal happiness. The decline of orthodox religion in the years following World War II has resulted in a surge of interest in all things spiritual – indeed, the thirst for spirituality, for the real meaning to life, has never been greater.

In 2007 an Australian daily newspaper, *The Sydney Morning Herald*, carried out a national survey on living standards and the results were staggering. Only 4 percent of respondents considered money and their financial situation as the most important factors in their happiness. Relationships and health status closely followed by religious/spiritual life topped the 'happiness' list – despite more than a decade of national economic prosperity.

There is no doubt at all that being happy and fulfilled at an inner level creates happiness and fulfillment on an outer level – in the physical world.

An understanding of the central role that Chakras play in achieving this personal quest for happiness is fundamental. Chakras provide us with an intimate blueprint to activate and balance life challenges, while remaining a powerful guide to the spiritual world.

When I compare one set of Chakras in one individual with another's, I can tell quite a lot about that person. More mature people, for instance, will have a larger set of chakras than a school child. The bigger the chakra, the more energy it will be able to hold. A large heart chakra will cause us to think a lot about compassion, giving and joy. A big Base Chakra will stimulate thoughts about material welfare, survival and the business of making money. Successful stockbrokers have powerful base chakras. When there is a lot of prayer or meditation, the Crown Chakra builds up. Physics, healers and other metaphysicians have large, upper chakras and can perceive subtle stimuli such as angels, spirit guides, energy currents and the like, whereas most stockbrokers, at the other end of the energy spectrum, cannot.

By changing the relative size of particular chakras, we change the things we focus on in life. In energy circles, this is called 'alignment' and is a fundamental tenet of the Law of Attraction that has been so popularized in the blockbuster book: 'The Secret'.

People with large, well-developed chakras are always successful in their chosen life path. Such individuals walk the world stage in whatever vocation or line of work they have chosen, some quietly, others noticeably. *There are no exceptions to this rule.*

I speak from personal experience when I say that when Chakras spin clockwise, they put energy into the body, but when they spin anti-clockwise, they draw energy out. When they become clogged with stress and/or emotional debris such as anger, fear, resentment and the like, this powerful spiritual network does not operate effectively. The rate at which the chakras spin slows down resulting in energy depletion that can be felt on the physical level as burnout, exhaustion or even depression.

There are many negative healers who are adept at altering the spin of these energy wheels to the detriment of the client and the empowerment of the healer. So, please be careful. Remember that you should feel good after a healing, never sick!

Many healers have described chakras as 'sorting posts' for

individual values and beliefs.

Unfortunately, from previous karmas and at each birth, we are indoctrinated with information, propaganda, and even other people's ideas. We spend years listening to the media, to politicians, to religious leaders... Each and every one of these people's chakras is charged with their own unique energies and individual code of beliefs. I have no doubt that some of what we have fed into us is undeniably good, wholesome and positive and this will make your chakras gather strength and flourish. But, I have to say, that quite a lot of this information is pretty toxic too. It can be harmful to you if you accept it and can make your chakras wither and even eventually stop altogether.

When we choose to believe negative things about ourselves and others we are actually causing our chakras to shrink and slow down. Chakra pollution is a very real occurrence.

However, if a chakra point is very under-activated (due to stress or negative emotions), often all that is required is to release the negative energy, clean up the chakra point and realign it so that it can spin clockwise once again.

A few years ago, I came across a woman who had battled the medical authorities for compensation for her disabled child for many years. Although she had retained her wonderful sense of humor (always a salvation point), the years of stress had taken their toll of her health. She was full of anger and had a tendency (not surprisingly) to succumb easily to despondency and despair. After a gap of some months, I met her again and this time could not help but notice the immense change to her entire person. She simply radiated joy, peace and, above all, wisdom. Noticing my surprise at her positive attitude to life, she told me what had happened. At the end of her tether over yet another legal tussle with hospital authorities, she had gone to see a faith healer. This man, a Holy man, talked to her for a little while and then placed his thumb quite firmly on the centre of her forehead (the Third eye chakra). Immediately, the woman was overcome with a tremendous sense of peace such as she had not known since childhood. She thanked him and then drove home, where she slept deeply and contentedly. The following day, she called her solicitor and informed him that she was dropping each and every one of her legal challenges.

The transformation, in this case, was brought about through the releasing of anger (one of the most toxic emotions known to man) and the realignment of her Third Eye Chakra, which governs the spirit. This chakra is the place where our true motivations are found and represents the level of consciousness that directs our actions and, indeed, our lives. What had happened to this woman? I believe that she had had an awakening to the real purpose of her life – caring for her child.

Chakra energy, when functioning in a pure and positive way, can be this powerful.

When chakras blossom, another world opens up to us.

Through our chakras we can access this world; we can become enriched and can gain a very real understanding of universal principles and patterns. We can each play our part in moving humanity forward and we will, as a matter of course, attract to us people with matching chakra energy patterns. By increasing our awareness of what we are broadcasting, in a sense, we can actually have a big effect on what we receive in life.

Change your chakras, and you can, quite literally, change your life.

The First Chakra – The Base Chakra

Location: The base of the spine or tailbone.

Color & Gemstone: Red. Ruby, Obsidian, Garnet.

Gland: Adrenals.

Sense: Smell.

Element: Earth.

Function: Known as the root or base chakra, this is your

grounding chakra – the chakra that connects you to the earth below your feet, enabling you to be present in the 'here and now'. It is linked to the healthy functioning of the lymphatic system, the skeletal system (teeth and bones), the prostate gland in men, the sacral plexus, the bladder and elimination systems as well as the lower extremities (legs, feet, ankles etc.). It also rules *the sense* of smell and is consequently intimately associated with human survival.

From the perspective of *consciousness,* basic survival and sexual energy is handled in this first chakra and when functioning harmoniously, the base chakra can give you sudden bursts of energy and strength when you need it. This chakra also reflects a person's connection with his/her mother as well as with the Earth. It is the most intimate expression for how you feel about being on the earth. Some people like to live near the sea, others in the mountains; some of us like to live in cities, whilst others prefer the countryside. By listening carefully to the energy from this chakra, you will find your own space, your own unique habitat, and your own way of living. This is the chakra that reminds us that we do not all march to the beat of the same drum....

Working with this powerful chakra can help you as an individual to create your own power centre and this is very, very important because your survival, your innate sense of *balance* with the world - and in the world - is determined right here at the base. If you are feeling 'out of sorts', not quite yourself etc. what you are really experiencing is a shift in the positive, energetic flow of this chakra.

When clearing up a negative magnetic energy field a few years back, I became accidentally 'infected' by some of the dark force. The first overt warning came quite suddenly – all of my clothes stank, my ankles swelled up and I succumbed to a heavy cold during which all of my bones literally ached day and night. I felt exhausted and really did not feel myself at all, but it was only when my hands began their telltale tingling that I finally 'switched on' to what had happened. I needed to realign the energy of this base chakra. As the negative energy was released, the base chakra began to spin clockwise again, my cold cleared up, my clothes stopped smelling, my ankles gradually stopped filling with fluid and I felt much more energized. Little by little, the tingling in my hands subsided and I was able to resume my work once more. In this instance, I had picked up someone else's negativity, which had created an imbalance in my life. By working hard to generate inner changes, the outer flow of energy was subsequently altered and restored.

The law of the jungle operates very powerfully with this the first chakra and when we feel a threat to our survival, we feel it here – at the base of the spine. Tension here is experienced as insecurity. When tension builds up, fear takes over. When fear is intensified, we experience terror. The old saying that we can feel bad things coming "in our water" is poignantly accurate. The two tiny adrenal glands sit atop of the kidneys – they are the first warning signs that something is wrong. A working knowledge of how to activate and to balance this chakra point liberates you from fear and nullifies anger and enables you to move onwards and upwards to the next rather pleasurable chakra.

When cords are attached at this point, physical and sexual energy may lower and the individual may even feel as if they are being 'punished' in some strange way, without really understanding why. At an extreme level, if attached over a long period of time at the base chakra some cords can even cause a person to lose the will to live. On a physical level, the immune system simply drains away and I often find that bowel cancer can be the painful inevitable result for people who have, quite literally, had other people's emotional debris dumped on them all their lives!

The Second Chakra – The Sacral Chakra
Location: The centre of the abdomen.
Color & Gemstone: Orange. Amber & carnelian.
Gland: Gonads.
Sense: Taste & appetite.
Element: Water.

Function: Here we have the Casanova of the Chakra world! The cardinal drive of this chakra power point is the parts of our consciousness concerned with food and sex. Sensual activities of whatever nature – sex, drugs, alcohol, food, the ability to feel attractive and to be able to attract things to you – are all emphasized by this wheel. It is fundamentally about the body's communication to the Being inside, about what the body wants and needs, and what it finds pleasurable.

Many of the world's greatest chefs whose love affair with food is so evident, have powerful second chakras. British chef, Gordon Ramsey, being a prime example.

An individual's ability to have children is also, not surprisingly, linked with the chakra which also governs the lumbar plexus.

A healthy, balanced abdominal centre, animated by magnetism, stimulated by arousal and yearning for fulfillment is the next logical step in life experience. We are now one step up from the critical survival stage present in the first chakra.

This second chakra is intimately entwined with the emotional body and our willingness to feel our emotions. When positively stimulated, it can be incredibly energizing. But, it does not always attract healthy experiences.

As a person's magnetism increases, he/she will attract greater opportunities to stray from the path of balance and harmony in life. For some this will mean an attraction to hedonistic pursuits and an indulgent lifestyle. The gossip magazines are literally teeming with tales of the incredible forays of the rich and famous. If only a fraction of this information were reality, these stories would be perfect examples of unbalanced abdominal chakras. All forms of addiction are attachments to the physical world, are very habit forming and can trap the individual in a cycle of unrelenting and ultimately miserable attempts to recreate transitory pleasures. There is no fulfillment when this chakra point is out of sync...

The development of a code of personal morals and values helps to hone the vitality of this chakra and to use its incredible power in a positive and transformative way that can continue to give personal delight and pleasure, but as part of a more *integrated* approach to life. Just as an imbalanced abdominal chakra can lead to jealousy, anger and fear, a balanced abdominal chakra can enrich our lives in a myriad of exquisite ways. Many of the world's greatest artists, writers and dancers whose genius borders on the frankly sensual - Michelangelo, D.H. Lawrence and the tactile sculptures of the late Barbara Hepworth - are prime examples of this chakra in perfect balance.

With the activation of this chakra, which is also known as the Muladhara or 'security centre', our human senses are awakened. We develop a deep appreciation of the world in which we live and the universe to which we are bound and we learn more about the Law of Attraction and magnetism.

It allows us to go forth into the world and to interact with others.

But, when cords are attached to this point, the individual may suffer from feelings of personal insecurity or may be prone to tears. It is here that we can see addictive behaviors begin – such as anorexia or, conversely, obesity. Creative people, such as writers, artists or musicians, may experience 'blocks' as their creative energy slows down. Physically, there may be kidney, bladder or lower back problems and later on, the beginnings of cancer of the prostate gland, testicles, ovaries or cervix.

The Third Chakra – The Solar Plexus
Location: Solar plexus.
Color & Gemstone: Yellow. Amber, topaz, yellow tourmaline & citrine.
Gland: The pancreas.
Sense: Eyesight.
Element: Fire, the sun.

Function: Perception is the keynote of this chakra. We have evolved from a state of sheer survival, have learnt to interact with others around us and now, as prana is awakened in this chakra point we are exposed to the sensations of power, control, freedom and the ease of being. This is the point at which we develop principles, ethics and beliefs. It is also the stage during which we establish boundaries in our life. The choice factor in life, our free will, becomes the primary motivator of the energy given to us by this solar plexus point.

We look at the world through the sense of the third chakra – at what is right and what is wrong. When we asked to 'stand up and be counted', this is the solar plexus chakra in glorious motion. Both the eyes and the face are governed by this point. This is how we literally see the world. It is also the face we show to the world.

The relationship a person has with fire, or the sun, also has its parallels in individual consciousness. Someone sensitive about the sun, for instance, will often have sensitive feelings about power, control or freedom.

The third chakra is all about *discrimination and self-control.*

Unbalanced third chakras can lead people to abuse positions of authority and can manifest in struggles for power. Just as the pancreas has the unenviable task of balancing the body's blood sugar levels, so this chakra reminds us all to balance chakra energy.

This is an incredibly powerful chakra, which can control and manipulate any incoming energy. Thus, physic attacks are invariably launched through the solar plexus. Dark energies often pierce the aura at this point and then spread rapidly throughout the entire individual's chakra system. The aim being to have total power over that person.

A cord at this energy wheel can prise the chakra open creating initially a feeling of confusion, followed by low self-esteem, a loss of confidence and a strange feeling of disempowerment. Worry, anxiety, fear and often anger soon set in, while physically the victim may experience exhaustion, pain in the abdomen, nausea, digestive upsets and blood disorders.

Working actively to protect this charka, as well as keeping a sense of perspective, a grip on reality, and knowing when "to pick a battle" and when to walk away, of keeping anger righteous as opposed to justified, are all part and parcel of maintaining the integrity of this plexus.

Wherever there is injustice in the world, whenever people feel a sense of repression, even when a person has trouble saying "no" and thus risks being taken advantage of by others – these are all evidence of imbalances in the third chakra. Energy is all around us every day – the way we chose to respond to this energy is critical. When you can balance the energy within yourself, you will find that the physical world will move into alignment with you. Sustaining equilibrium throughout the subtle and universal chakra system requires focus, love, courage and joy.

This is the lesson of the Third Chakra.

The Fourth Chakra – The Heart

Location: The centre of the chest

Color & Gemstone: Emerald green & rose quartz, aventurine.

Gland: Thymus Gland.

Sense: Touch.

Element: Air.

Function: I have to admit that this is my favourite chakra point – partly because I have such a large heart chakra myself, but also because when we talk in spiritual terms about the "awakening of the heart" what we are essentially talking about is opening ourselves up to the endless possibility of universal love.

For now, we are at last ready to experience the magnificence of the greatest of all divine blessings - love.

So much is spoken about love in the world today. The lonely hearts columns of newspapers and magazines, the profundity of internet 'chat rooms', even the sex industry – all are cogs in the universal wheel that spins ever on in the search for love.

Yet, as the heart chakra, so poignantly reminds us, true love comes from *within.* It is the joyful awakening of the dawn of wisdom, peace and ever-lasting joy. It is what we were created for. Teaching us about love was central to Christ's mission, whilst the 13th century Indian poet and mystic Rumi reminds us that: "Everything in the Universe is within you, ask all from yourself". Tibetans see the awakening of the heart chakra as a major step to selflessness – one of the first stages on the path to enlightenment.

Love, literally, makes the world go round. It is the 'heart' of humanity.

The sense of touch is intimately connected to this chakra. Hugging is a heart chakra activity. When we hug someone, we become aware of what the other person is feeling inside his/her body and they, for their part, are equally aware of what is going on inside you! There is a tremendous sense of relating to that person. When an individual is sensitive about being touched, this indicates heart chakra sensitivity. Difficulties in breathing or with the lungs, the organs of air, also indicate tension in the heart chakra. In a way, a person's relationship with the element of air mirrors their relationship with love.

When the energy of the heart chakra begins to flow, compassion is awakened. A great sense of interconnectedness takes over and peace and harmony are very much the norm. The more time spent in harmony, the more harmony you will attract into your life. You will also bring out this quality in others. But connection to the source of love – the Supreme Being – is essential to maintain the free flowing of this chakra energy. If you cannot drink from the source (God), you will not be replenished and may well end up feeling exhausted and depleted.

When love has other *needs* attached to it – such as sex, security or power, the heart chakra can become unbalanced.

A negative cord here can result in feelings of being emotionally drained, of being jealous and possessive. There are often problems in relationships with others especially over issues to do with trust, fidelity and acceptance. When affected, the entire respiratory and circulatory systems become weakened.

Love that is based on attachment is limited and all too often brings the person nothing but sorrow and irritation. When the heart chakra is out of alignment, love becomes a very dominating and controlling form of emotion. It can be unbearable.

It is said that AIDS is fundamentally a deep problem with an individual's perceptions of love. Interestingly, the Thymus gland controls the immune system. This gland is governed by energies from the heart chakra. If an AIDS sufferer feels that their lifestyle separates them from those they love – often because of societal judgments, the heart chakra does not spin positively, slows down and the more negative emotions from the first, second and third chakras tend to dominate. Survival and the pursuit of hedonistic pleasures cloud the true beauty of the heart chakra. Learning to find spiritual nourishment once more may well be the key to finding a panacea for many AIDS sufferers and their families.

Diana, the late Princess of Wales, had an enormous heart chakra. Despite the unhappiness of her own private relationships and her personal problems, she had so much love to give. She gave that love to the world. All those individuals whose lives she touched felt the radiance of her heart chakra.

Australian environmentalist, Steve Irwin, whose untimely

death so shocked the world, was another individual whose heart chakra was large and luminous. His passion for the natural world radiated from his heart.

When you love others in such a powerful way that their happiness becomes such a focal point in your own existence, this is the heart chakra in action. On a grander scale, the heart chakra reminds us that we are all interconnected, that our hearts literally beat as one.

When the heart chakra is spinning positively, you give freely to others *from your heart.* When it is out of alignment, you feel exhausted in mind and body. Most heart patients are often breathless and tire easily. This is no mere medical symptom. This is heart chakra imbalance. Reconnecting with nature and the Light of the World allows you to draw in God's beauty and love. You will be replenished. Individual love, universal love and compassionate love are the three major ventricles of the heart chakra.

But please remember that a broken heart can be healed. By restoring balance to the first three chakras, the heart centre can once again be opened up to the flow of divine energy – the pure, white light of goodness. Opening to the heart chakra changes your life in extraordinary ways and it is never the same again....

The Fifth Chakra – The Throat

Location: Base of the throat.

Color & Gemstone: Sky blue. Aquamarine, celestite and crysocola.

Gland: Thyroid gland.

Sense: Hearing.

Element: The Junction of the physical and the spiritual worlds.

Function: I call this chakra the 'Opera Singer' of the universe! For, it is no mere coincidence that opera singers have well-developed and powerful throat chakras. So, too, do great orators, writers and theatre actors. When the throat chakra is working perfectly, all the world is literally a stage!

This, the fifth chakra is the centre for expressive communication as well as making and keeping commitments. A by-word for this energy point is: "Ask and ye shall receive" as all aspects of expression come under its control. Not everyone can sing at La Scala, so this chakra is about expressing your individuality as a mother, teacher, dustman or gardener...

As Pranic energy flows upwards from the heart centre, we are challenged to find our voice and to "speak the Truth". When this energy takes over, many people actually experience it as a real sensation – as a quickening, or as "butterflies" that can make them feel a bit nervous. Some individuals, unprepared for the encompassing surge of throat chakra energy can get overwhelmed by it and end up feeling anxious and out of control with it. The key is, of course, to allow this energy to flow and to move into step with it – rather like learning new dance steps. When you merge with the fifth chakra power point, you begin listening to your intuition. This is the ultimate state of grace, the universal abundance bestowed on you at the moment of conception.

Elementally, this chakra represents the crossroads between the physical world and the spirit. It represents the matrix on which physical reality manifests and upon which spiritual energy soars.

When positively aspected, creative energy flows freely from you to others. The light of wisdom shines through.

This chakra also controls the neck, arms and hands, so "Writer's Block" and "Stage Fright" are all too familiar at this level. Working with energy healers to bring all the previous chakras into positive alignment can overcome these hurdles.

Unbalanced throat chakra energies can manifest in feelings of aggression. Here we have the person who stands stubbornly by his/her opinions. This is the "Mr/Ms. No" of the chakra world.

The non-conformist rebel who, rather than listen to another person's point of view, is so attached to his own, that he becomes blind to the universal Truth: unconditional love.

When cords are attached at this level, it is often with the purpose of letting the other person do the talking for you! Issues of trust, of being heard or even of being believed can come into play. At worst, a negative attachment here can block the flow of creative expression and can soon lead to depression. Physically, there may be speech or hearing difficulties, even thyroid gland dysfunction as well as pain in the neck and shoulder region.

Many great story-tellers have highly evolved throat chakras, but so too do many con-artists, whose primary motivation is not to elaborate on the truth to entertain others and maybe to convey an important message, but rather to take from others to enrich themselves. The gift of the gab can work both ways!

Known as Anahata or the Living love Centre, this power centre represents our relationship with our own space and the world stage on which we all stride. It opens us to the next stage in energy awareness, the move towards God.

The Sixth Chakra – The Third Eye
Location: Centre of the Forehead.
Color & Gemstone: Indigo/Midnight Blue. Indigo tourmaline, Fluorite.
Gland: Pituitary Gland.
Sense: Extra Sensory Perception (ESP).
Element: Inner Sound.

Function: This chakra is linked with the deep inner level of Being we call Spirit and with what we consider spirituality and the spiritual perspective. In western tradition, the Third All-Seeing Eye is representative of the subconscious or unconscious. To eastern beliefs this is Visuddha, the seat of higher mental and intuitive abilities. At this level we can engage in spirit-to-spirit communication through clairvoyance (inner sense of vision), clairaudience (inner sense of hearing) and clairsentience (inner sense of touch). Through the Third Eye, the physical world is seen as a manifestation of co-creation. A sense of the deeper meaning of life is unfurled as we open up to the energy of the sixth chakra point.

This is the power centre of the Prophets, who saw the world and everyone in it as part of God's creation. It is the Tao (or 'Way') and the attainment of Mindfulness in Buddhism. The essence of universal life force is experienced here.

For most people the energy of the Third Eye is experienced as intuition, as knowing when something is not quite as it should be – even if, to the naked eye, everything appears to be as normal. Intuition is an inner alarm system that warns of imminent peril ahead. By listening to our Third Eye, we can avoid many potential danger spots. Those individuals who instinctively left their desks and dashed down the stairs as the Twin Towers of the World Trade Centre collapsed saved their lives. Those who, by choice, remained in their offices perished.

One of the biggest blessings about being open and receptive to the energy from this field is that you can eventually learn to "read" your own intuition – to know if you are feeling fear, inspiration, faith, disillusionment or creativity.

The danger point with a negatively aspected Third Eye is to disengage from the potency of intuition and to disbelieve in any other realm than that of the purely physical. This is simply asking for trouble. By ignoring something that your body can actually feel (eg: fear) or even see (eg: an entity), you can inadvertently create havoc in your own life and the lives of those you love.

The potency of the Third Eye chakra can also be turned deliberately against mankind. According to Grail expert Trevor Ravenscroft, when Hitler's Third Eye was opened during a special satanic ceremony, his mind became so tortured, that it released a steady torrent of rage and torture at the entire human race and allowed his body to be completely taken over by the most foul of demonic entities. (3)

When someone cords here at the Third Eye, they may wish to intimidate you mentally or interfere with the dynamics of your spiritual microcosm. Nightmares, telepathic thoughts, various "odd" ideas may find their way into your sub-conscious. You may have problems meditating, imagining or even working psychically. There may be feelings of confusion, disorientation, even depression. On a physical level, there may be constant headaches or problems with eyesight, even hormonal dysfunction (as the Pituitary Gland is affected). At the extreme end of the spectrum, a cord at this energy point can cause dyslexia, delusion, learning difficulties even brain tumors.

Allowing one's imagination to run amok is often a strong signal that the Third Eye is out of alignment. Unfortunately, a lot of misguided and devious mystics are adept at manipulating this power centre in others, so watch out! If your body is urging you to stay, but your instinct says: "Run like Hell!" get running! Now!

One of the greatest joys of working with Third Eye energies is the ability to read your own private energy levels. Often I will feel my energy field expanding and glowing when I am in a particularly spiritual environment (a Place of Worship, a beautiful garden etc.). But I can also sense a tightening and slowing down of chakra energies when fear, danger or darkness is experienced. Finding inspiration and being able to be still in the presence of God is enormously uplifting during these times. When dowsing a field of negative energy, for example, I will focus on bringing Light, laughter and joy back into the distressed area. The Third Eye chakra is a wonderful beacon for tapping into this energy.

When you have opened up to the power of this chakra, you are ready for the next and final step....

The Seventh Chakra – The Crown Chakra
Location: Top of the Head.
Color & Gemstone: Violet (or white) & Clear Quartz.
Gland: Pineal Gland.
Sense: Empathy, unity, experiencing another person's situation.
Element: Inner Light.

Function: This, the final stage of chakra development, is about the merging of the self with the Supreme Being. This is the attainment of the Spiritual Path that commands the letting go of all attachments in order to merge with God and his unique purpose for you. This is what you were born for – what God has called you to do.

Just as the Base Chakra reveals our connection with Mother Earth, the Crown Chakra shows our relationship with Our Father in heaven. Interestingly, it also mirrors our connection with our biological father and this subsequently becomes the model for our relationship with authority, and, ultimately, of course, with God. In the purest sense of the word, this power point, through which Kundalini soars upwards and outwards into the Divine, represents the level of the soul.

When you experience a sense of separation from your father, the crown chakra is closed and an overwhelming feeling of isolation and aloneness dominates. It is as if you are in a shell, having difficulty feeling contact with the people around you. Thought processes too justify and maintain this sense of isolation and of being alone.

This chakra started the process of receiving energy from God, so it is fitting that in the final moments of mortal life that this gateway also completes the pranic cycle: the universal energy that sparked physical life is surrendered back to the universe. In a word, we go back to God.

It is now as this chakra point comes into its own that we

realize that everything we perceive is merely an extension of our own consciousness. The entire life process is seen very much as a spiritual experience. Here we have a glimpse of the Enlightenment so courted by Buddhists and which is felt through deep prayer and meditation. Inner Light is experienced as a point of consciousness glowing with intelligence.

When we open up to the potency of the Crown Chakra we see life through the eyes of God. We see as God sees. But such a state is a fleeting experience at best for the few fortunate humans who can engage fully with God, and is usually the result of living a sacred and holy life. When you experience life at this level, it requires *total surrender.*

Here we have the holy men or hermits, and the monks who live in splendid isolation away from the world, yet in the world. But living a life from the perspective of the seventh chakra is also possible for many ordinary men and women. The one demand this energy places on you is giving way to God's will. This is God's purpose for you in literal physical action.

When St. Francis of Assisi gave up the life of an idle rich young man for the austere demands of the life of a hermit, his father disowned him publicly. Yet St. Francis, we are told, could live his life no other way. By surrendering to God's mission for him, he gave up freely the tangible world of materialism for the infinite rewards of living a spiritual life. He found great contentment and inner peace. He also found purpose to his life. But his choice was not a sacrifice. It was a willing and completely conscious choice.

So many people try to balance the demands of the material world (supporting loved ones etc.) with what they would really rather do. How many of us know of the artist who holds down a mundane job to 'keep the wolf from the door' when this individual would much rather be painting all day? Having the courage to let go of material attachments and to trust in a higher power is never an easy step for people to take, but I am struck time and again of how when we align ourselves with the potency of this chakra point that God actually does provide for us all – just like he does for the birds of the air....

For many years, as a reporter I specialized in healthcare and scientific matters when my interest had always lain within the realm of the spiritual. When I became a dowser, I no longer had to hide my feelings and thoughts about energy, but it took many years before I had the courage to actually write openly about such things. In the past, getting manuscripts and features published on health or science issues had never been an easy task. I was frequently criticized for being 'too religious', 'too uncomfortably moralistic' and so on. Yet discussing the spiritual perspective of human health and of the scientific world was what I clearly enjoyed writing about. At the grand age of 47 years, I finally surrendered to this feeling. To my astonishment, my features on spirituality and energy healing were snapped up and my income grew steadily. By letting go and 'letting God', we give spirit the opportunity to get involved in our lives and our lives are never the same again....

I see this lesson of the seventh chakra being played out in so many other people's lives again and again. Some struggle to accommodate this change by trying desperately to exercise strict control of their lives and often, of everyone else around them too. Fear takes hold and love cannot grow in such soil. But when we allow the energy of the seventh charka to flow freely, we evolve. It really is all about living our life for the greater glory of God – as a parent, teacher, artist, or religious – whatever path we are guided by spirit to walk.

But one word of warning must be sounded – if the path that you opt to walk in this life does not move you closer to your higher self or to God please be very careful. By being still and waiting for the *real thing* in your life, I am confident that your unique path will be revealed to you in time.

Despite its many glorious revelations, this chakra is also a risky place to be unbalanced. It can lead to total disassociation with the world around you and a very real failure to play your role in that world. When this unfortunate state occurs, the lower chakras are almost always out of alignment.

It is also here that we see the Universal Law of Attraction taken grossly out of context.

Many dedicated followers of this Law treat the cosmos as if it were a personal shopping catalogue to thumb through at leisure and to select from at will. Some contemporary teachings lean to the power of creating your own life, as if you, as an individual, were a god. This is the power of the ego taking over and is the most glaring instance of chakra imbalance that I have ever seen.

As humans we are made *in the image of God.* But we *are not God.* We have free will – a choice between good and evil. This is quintessentially our choice. But we do not know more about our needs than God. The rich man who pursues riches for the sake of it, is never, if ever, happy with his life.

Although it is relatively rare to find cords attached to this chakra, they do sometimes happen and often, I find, that person doing the cording is quite deliberately intending to disrupt the victim's link with the spirit world. Often, too, the perpetrator wants to tap into the wealth of spiritual knowledge that the person may have. When cords are attached here, the victim may feel a sense of alienation from the world around them, as though they have been 'cut off' which, in a sense, they have! There may be problems linking up to beings of higher vibrational reality such as Angels, Ascended Masters etc. On a more mundane level, even praying can become problematic. With this kind of attack, headaches and memory problems become pronounced and, as the Pineal Gland is affected, insomnia and problems with the body's central nervous system may manifest.

When it is in perfect balance, the seventh chakra is all about taking the 'I' out of the 'Ego' and not making attempts to control the flow of your life – always a very dangerous game.

It is White Light because it is the most subtle element of which the entire Universe is made. The Crown Chakra is all about knowing God.

In so many ways, chakras are the embodiment of spiritual energy whose actions are clearly visible in the physical world. By restoring clear, radiant energy to this incredibly vibrant system, miracles can and do happen. Broken hearts mend, speech is restored, cancer dissipates and life is lived to the greater glory of God.

MUDRAS & HEALING HANDS

"That day, we set a seal on their mouths, but their hands will speak to us, and their hands bear witness to all that they did."
Prophet Mohammed Sahib, The Koran.

All chakras are exposed to wavelengths of information and are connected via the meridian network to 'contact points' on the surface of the skin.

In ancient eastern texts, when Kundalini awakening occurs, a flow of energy in the form of cool vibrations from the hands is experienced and the various chakras can actually be felt on parts of the hands or fingers.

The positioning of our hands during prayerful meditation is known as *Mudras* – a cornerstone of yogic practices that have been used around the world for centuries. Statues and artworks throughout the East clearly depict a range of mudras. Different hand positions have helped to identify the various forms of Buddha for example and they feature extensively in the artworks of almost every single ancient culture and religion throughout the region. A Sanskrit word meaning 'sign' or 'seal', mudras have been described in great detail in traditional religious texts such as the *Tantra Shastra, Upansana Shastra* and *Nritya Shastra.* It is widely thought that they date back to Lord Shiva, the Hindu god of destruction and regeneration and there are many paintings of Shiva with his hands in one of the many mudra positions.

Paintings of the Sacred Heart of Jesus depict Christ with His right hand raised to shoulder height (the *abhaya* mudra or gesture of fearlessness) and with His left hand at the centrre of His chest where the heart chakra is located. This is a very powerful gesture used by the Children of God, the Elect, to communicate with God.

But mudras are so much more than aesthetic gestures – for they serve as an electrical contact point providing direct access into a chakra zone through one or two meridians manipulating and redirecting prana through the hands and fingers back into the body. Mudras are quite literally healing hands in motion.

The five elements of fire, water, earth, air and sky or ether are represented by our fingers and thumb. The thumb represents fire *(agni),* the forefinger air *(vayu),* the middle finger ether *(akash),* the ring finger earth *(prithvi),* and the little finger water *(jal).*

Each finger is linked to a primary chakra. The mudra, for instance, to access the root chakra is the thumb and index or first finger. The second chakra is accessed as the second finger and thumb and so on. Upon completion of the fourth finger and thumb mudra, the first finger and thumb are reused to access the next higher, or fifth chakra. The order is as follows:

Finger	**Chakra**
Index or First Finger	Root chakra
Second Finger	Sacral Chakra
Third Finger	Solar Plexus Chakra
Fourth Finger	Heart Chakra

In this order, the first finger now accesses the fifth chakra

First Finger	Throat Chakra
Second Finger	Third Eye Chakra

Third Finger	Crown Chakra

Mudras can not only stimulate a different state of consciousness, it is believed that they can invoke the presence of God. The mudra of prayer is that of the hands facing one another in front of the body, fingers extended with the tips and palms touching each other. Taught as the preferred form of prayer in many Christian traditions, what is often overlooked is the actual *reason for this mudra.* When each of the fingertips touches those of the opposite hand, it completes the energy circuits along which prana flows and opens access to the associated chakra zones and grids *at the same time.* The contact of the palm chakras, the large chakras in the centre of each hand, enhances the flow of energy-information-light to other body parts or indeed to other humans. When we clench our hands together instead of pressing them palm-to-palm we are in fact crossing all our meridian points – which is very confusing for the dynamics of human energy!

Throughout history, humans have been called upon to lift up their hands in prayer. Romans used to stand with their arms raised in prayer, while early Christians would often pray with their arms fully extended in acknowledgment of Christ's position on the Cross. In Timothy 1 2:8 humans are actively called upon to "lift up holy hands in prayer". During the sacrament of the Eucharist at Catholic Masses, the priest lifts his hands in prayer and supplication to God.

The reason why this is such an effective means of energy transfer is this: each finger transmits its own frequency directing the flow of energy in silent conversation with God. It is now, during prayerful contemplation, that we can alter not only our mood and attitude, but we can deepen our perception and our awareness of the miracle of creation.

Through the use of mudras, energy healers can liberate energy that has been trapped in the body to cure ailments ranging from a simple earache or stiff neck to heart disease and cancer. Practice of the mudras on a regular basis can cure insomnia, arthritis and memory degeneration.

AURAS – THE COMMUNION WITH THE PHYSICAL

'Aura: subtle emanation, atmosphere diffused by or attending person, place etc. From the Greek = breeze, breath.'
Oxford English Dictionary

The combined expression of all of the wheels of light (Chakras) makes up your *aura* – the radiations of light energy that sheath the subtle body. In fact a further five major subtle bodies are connected to the physical one that we wear.

Larger than the flesh and blood hardware, the energy body is actually denser the closer it is to the human body. As its layers spread further out, these subtle sheaths become lighter, more translucent and shimmering. Every sentient being has these multidimensional bodies of dazzling light around them and they are clear indicators of health and well-being. Although psychics and clairvoyants can see auras automatically, with practice anyone can learn to read auras if they are dedicated enough and patient.

Whereas the physical body requires food and oxygen to survive and is controlled essentially by the mind, the subtle body needs a 'diet' of soul food, or prana, to thrive. Unlike the physical, the energy body is not curtailed by the degenerative processes of aging or disease, although it too is susceptible to negative and draining energies that sap its vitality which, in turn, impact on the status of the physical shell.

Each person's energy field is unique and mirrors that person's own vibratory level. But plants, animals and even inanimate objects that have picked up energy from their environment or the living creatures in it, possess auras, too.

Auras can be seen most easily in dim light. They appear to the eye (and to special cameras) as a field of colored light that differs for each individual. The aura of a creature can also change throughout the day as energy levels and moods alter. Different colors indicate different things and health, emotions, stress and personality are all clearly marked on a person's energy body.

At birth we are linked closely with the body, mind and auras of our mothers. The general consensus among experts in this field is that this auric bond between a mother and her child remains for somewhere between 7 to 10 years. Thus, mothers need to keep this tangible connection in mind when allowing unnecessary separations from their children. If long periods are spent apart, the children, as well as the mother, will experience an energy drain. The same can be said for fathers, but *because of the long period of time a child spends in the womb feeding off its mother's auric energy, a bond is created that can be damaging if broken too soon.*

The health diet of the auric body remains *love.* Negative emotions such as anger, resentment, and jealousy may seem invisible to the outside world, but these emotions are not hidden from everybody. To people gifted with auric reading skills, your emotions, if negative, look like a great big dirty stain on your shirt! It is so important to watch that negative thoughts or feelings do not overwhelm you. They may not be as harmless as you think! Simply being aware of the existence of your aura is critical too – believe me there are certain unscrupulous people who are also adept at reading auras and who can sense if your energy field is strong, weak or disabled – and this is when BIG trouble can start.

As mentioned earlier, *psychic vampires* simply love to drain auras, rather than release energy and this is one key way that you will know when you are being psychically attacked. The human body is more than 70 per cent water and water is a potent energy source. When you are in the presence of low astral entities, you will feel a disturbance not just in your spiritual body, but physically you will also become very thirsty, you may even get a sudden sharp headache. Headaches are often caused by a simple lack of water and when someone has drained your energy, your physical body will send out a signal for water – and plenty of it! Psychic vampires simply love to cause arguments as well and are adept at generating conflict that often manifests in vigorous and exhausting outbursts of red-hot rage and anger.

When I first started working as a junior reporter in London in the late '70s, I came across an editor who was extremely adept at pitting couples against each other. Having stirred things up, Max used to sit back in his comfortable armchair and enjoy the drama unfolding in front of him in the newsroom. The angry couple were left feeling exhausted for days afterwards, but I always used to think it odd that as the couple tired, Max seemed to grow in the most amazing strength. It was as if he had been given a shot of adrenalin – which, I suppose, in a way, he had. He had, you see, quite literally 'fed off' the negative energy he had created.

There are more psychic vampires about that you could possibly imagine, so it is critical to hone your aura daily, cleanse it of toxic debris and surround yourself with love, laughter and joy *every single day of your life.*

Shielding techniques can be extremely useful in deflecting leech attempts. Protecting yourself by throwing up a wall of brilliant white light around you (think of 'Star Wars') acts like a force field. White energy radiating from your person is not well used by psychic vampires, though I have known of some who can tolerate it just long enough to invade your space and sap your energy. By sitting with your arms folded and your legs firmly together, being sure to keep both feet on the ground to make contact with the earth, you can create a closed circuit between yourself and the earth. Your energy can only move through you and back to its source. The parasite is thus shut out.

I have personally known of some lower energy beings though who can infiltrate churches and other sacred places of worship.

It is important to remember that these beings can only do these things, if we *permit them.* The biggest invitation is, of course, ignorance of negative energies and an inability by the vast majority of people to read the signs of negative psychic energy – until it is too late...

In today's environment of consumerism and cynicism, even some priests and church leaders can be dismissive of these lower energy forms, despite their training and the many references in the Bible and other religious texts to demonic entities, and this can create an opening just wide enough for negative energy forms to slip in.

When I had occasion to remind a religious leader recently that Jesus had taken several demons out of Mary Magdalene, this gentleman looked at me in complete disbelief. Maybe he needed to hear this. Yet the Bible does not lie and contains numerous references in it to lower astral entities.

Often I will sense the presence of negative energy through my physical body and I can feel "out of sorts", not quite myself, even sick. If the negative entity is really dark, I will feel a profound pain in my third eye charka. It is important to remember though that everyone is different and we all respond in individual ways to negative energy. My husband tends to get snappish, cross and irritable. Other people may feel sleepy, experience low energy levels, have frequent accidents or smell repulsive odors. *These are all critical warning signs that something is wrong.*

The most effective defense against such negative feelings and influences is of course, a positive attitude, a determination to focus on worthwhile goals, and an avoidance of contact or dabbling with the paranormal by the uninitiated. Healing damaged auras and strengthening weakened ones is a highly specialized job. But when you become more attuned to the world in which you live and when you learn to meditate on a daily basis, your aura will grow in strength and light and you will eventually be able to strengthen it yourself.

Studying the colors that you don't see, as well as the ones you can see in your aura, is also tremendously important. If the color red is missing from your subtle body for example, you will need to look at ways to improve your health and the zest for life. Cancer suffers almost invariably lack this color. By tuning into the colors of the chakras and the vibrations of the missing colors, health can be restored once again.

A beautifully balanced, well-rounded aura is one that has as many colors as possible and ensures a balanced body, mind and soul and is truly a joy to behold!

Above all, a healthy aura should look like an egg.

Any breaks, misshapen spots, tears or other flaws can indicate inner emotional, mental, physical or spiritual problems. Grey or black areas that cover certain parts of the body are indicators of hidden illnesses and should be dealt with by professional healers.

Occasionally stories of auric invasion do make newspaper headlines, though it is always doubtful if the journalist concerned is really aware of what is actually going on.

On April 14, 1956, 'The Times' reported that modern science in the shape of an iron lung, had rescued a young Australian Aborigine from what would have been without any doubt an agonizing death caused, the newspaper claimed by witchcraft. The youth, Lya Wulumu, had been flown to Darwin Hospital by the Yirrkala Methodist Mission, having been found ill and convinced that he was slowly being crushed to death by an invisible giant snake. First his feet became paralyzed, then his knees and thighs; he was unable to swallow and finally began to struggle for breath as though the coils of an enormous serpent were indeed crushing his rib cage.

A few days earlier it was discovered that the boy had incurred the anger of tribal elders and womenfolk of the Gubamwingu tribe for an offence against tribal laws, and had had a death curse put on him in the form of a 'singing ceremony'.

This story intrigued me as it showed clearly that aboriginals believe that if a person has met with a serious accident or has died, that he or she has become the victim of black magic. In this instance, black magic was a very dark psychic attack. By performing a ritual (a rite on a footprint, or burning and stabbing a small image of the victim, or pointing a bone or stick at the intended victim to the accompaniment of action and chant), the aura of the individual is quite literally stabbed and the chakras start to spin backwards as a negative magnetic energy field is set up which, in turn, impacts greatly on the victim's physical health and well being.

Bone pointing releases a force that implants a spiritual bone or splinter into the victim's auric body without leaving a mark on the skin.

On his travels throughout Asia, English author Somerset Maugham met with many examples of this type of attack and gives a first-hand account of a similar incident in his collection of short stories *'The Casuarina Tree'* where a returning expatriate has a death curse put on him by local Malay villagers. The unfortunate man hiccupped to death....

But wherever harm can be invoked, healing is also possible.

And I am making a very powerful statement when I say that when you can work with your energy field and everything within it, you have the power within you to heal. This is the power that was given to each and every one of us by God.

Unfortunately, western society preaches the mantra of *delegation* as opposed to personal responsibility. If your car has broken down, you take it to the mechanic. If your body is sick, you book an appointment for the GP. But the GP is trained only in the 'mechanics' of the human body, not in sustaining the spiritual body. The alcoholic executive whose habit is a mask for personal despair, or the depressed housewife who longs to be appreciated and loved for herself are just two examples where drug therapy alone is ultimately destined for failure because the very real spiritual problems of the patients have not been addressed.

When these other higher vibrational issues are also given attention, vital creative energies can be channeled in more balanced ways. The result is a return to full health.

The distribution of energy commences at the spiritual or causal level. This then creates an organizational matrix at various other levels in an individual's aura.

The following is a listing of the main human energy fields:

The Etheric Body is the bridge between the physical body and connecting higher energies and helps with the control of the physical or material body. The etheric sheath is an energy matrix which shapes and anchors the physical matter of the body's tissues.

In size and in shape, it is very similar to the material body. It follows the human outline carefully and extends only about 6 mms (roughly a quarter of an inch) from the skin of the material body.

Invisible to the human eye, psychics and healers see this outline as a faint bluish shadow. The Etheric Body in turn consists of a range of three sheaths – vital, mental and intellectual.

The Astral Body is the bridge between the lower, denser vibrations of the physical body and the finer vibrations of the spiritual plane.

In addition to *sensing* external stimuli through the five senses, this is the sheath that actively *craves* specific things, while at the same time *alerting* the body to fundamental survival instincts. It is here in this sheath, for instance, that we actually experience the sensations of hunger, cold, thirst, pain and pleasure etc. first.

The Astral Body is intimately associated with the Heart Chakra and is the transforming crucible through which all energy must pass when going from one world to another. It is said that all spiritual energy must pass through the 'fire' of the heart before being transformed into the lower physical energies. Physical energies in their turn also have to pass through the 'fire' of the heart chakra before becoming spiritual energies.

The 'Sacred Heart' of Christ is not just a pretty picture. It is a portal for Divine Love in so many exceptional ways.

It is on this level that we find ideas (the intellect) as well as the experience we call *astral travel,* known to many science fiction fans as the space-time-continuum.

Among the most difficult of all skills to master, astral travel is essentially a process by which the spiritual body is projected into the astral plane from our physical plane. Distortions and shifts in our present time period are common when undergoing this experience. Time travel or finding yourself in another period and geographic location is not uncharacteristic for astral projection. A few minutes in the physical world can stretch to hours, days or even longer on the astral plane. Dion Fortune has given reliable accounts of astral travel in her many works and notes that you can find yourself in many strange lands with different physical laws or no boundaries at all.

Reality and unreality blend into one.

Seen by psychics as light-blue to grey in color and extending for up to 6 cms or 2 inches in width, this is the sheath that survives death as a ghost or spirit, is not subject to gravity and can pass easily through dense objects.

Responsible for creating bodily warmth, when this sheath detaches at death and hovers above the body, the body grows cold as death approaches.

NDEs or Out of Body Experiences (OBEs) are also felt at this energetic level due to partial separation of the astral and physical bodies.

Although during an OBE you are not technically in the astral plane, you are "on the border" between our world and the astral world.

Such close proximity results in a continued awareness of time and space. Information imparted after an OBE or a NDE is often reliable, as you are consciously hearing or seeing even when your physical body is incapable of receiving information (ie: clinically dead) or your physical body is too far away (in another room, for example) to receive information about the situation.

The Mental Body is concerned with every single aspect of the mind including *conscious mental functioning* where the qualities of thought, deliberation and reason come into play.

This sheath is manifested by the various thought-forms and ideas created by the mind. "I think therefore I am" is especially true at this level.

Extending for up to 13 cms or 6 inches from the boundaries of the physical body, it can be seen as a glow surrounding the head.

The Celestial Body is associated with the 'higher' emotional aspects of the spirit and is also known as the *intuitive level.* When we intuitively know our connection to the universe, when we see light and love in everything that exists, we have entered the realms of the Celestial Body.

The Causal Body is the sheath of universal consciousness. When we experience the reality of a oneness with All That Is, we are tuned to the level of the Causal Body.

This sheath, together with the Celestial, forms the higher self and is the seat of the permanent soul. It also reflects all of the experiences and events that the soul has ever had. The entire life plan of the individual is held at this level, which is the last level related to this incarnation. Interestingly, this body adopts the same sex as your physical body during any given incarnation.

Beyond the realm of the Causal lies the **Cosmic Plane** – a stage that cannot be experienced from the confines of the ego. Here we find the union of the soul with God and the final testament to the infinity of time and space within which the soul dwells.

Although most auric readers have only been able to discern some portions of the human energy field, when we, as individuals, learn to see beyond our own aura and learn to trust the very gentle messages we get as various people move into and out of our personal energy field, we become aware that we are now ready to take the next step in the evolution of mankind.

SLEEP, DREAMS & THE EVOLUTION OF THE SOUL

"To understand this One-essence is to be released from all entanglements"
Hsin Hsin Ming: Sengstan's Verses on the Faith Mind.

The ultimate state of altered awareness for all humans is, of course, the dream state.

Rest is as important for the spiritual body as it is for the physical. When we sleep each night, our spirit leaves our body and enters the realms of the universe where it is recharged with cosmic energy.

The subtle body is connected by delicate silvery threads of unlimited elasticity and is linked etherically to the physical body at the solar plexus and at the crown chakra.

While we sleep, our spirit can do one of three things: it will either stay with our body, hover alongside it or else it can travel far away to other places on the earth or to other dimensions. Astral travel for the spirit is not bound by distance or time.

While you sleep your spiritual body can travel to other lands, explore the depths of the oceans, soar across mountain ranges, visit other stars, or even cross the galaxy. Have you ever had a dream where you felt yourself falling or flying through the air, then woke up with a sudden shock? The 'shock' that you have actually experienced is the sensation of the subtle body quite literally dropping back into the physical body. Sometimes you can wake up with a shudder or actually give a lurch in bed as these two energy fields merge.

During our waking hours we work on our life purpose, but

while we are asleep we are quite literally in communication with the other aspects of our energy field and the subtle body is busy working at spiritual tasks that are just as valid as those of our conscious state.

Sleep is known to be the filter for the day's activities. But sleep is much more than a mere processing mechanism. As waves of subtle energy interact with other waves we begin to influence the world we call 'reality' – as Nikola Tesla's oscillation machines so clearly demonstrated more than a century ago.

In recent years the western scientific concept of 'solid' has surrendered to the idea that solid matter is an illusion. When viewed from this perspective, reality appears to be nothing more than a series of rapid bursts of energy pulsating at specific rates manifesting along predictable and consistent waves.

It is these patterns (waves of energy) that our brain 'sees' and strings together to produce the perception of a solid, continuous event – the so-called 'reality'.

Indigenous peoples around the world have said for centuries that our world is a world of illusion – that everything we experience in this world while 'alive' is the product of pure thought and, as such, is not real. Ancient texts caution us that our world is actually the world of a dream.

When we consider the realm of the dream state from this perspective, dreams provide the spark to the mental and psychic processes that will bring them into the world of physicality. Through dreams we can draw on a vast body of universal knowledge, we can choose events that we wish to make physical or 'real' and we can gain and share much wisdom.

The great Swiss psychologist Carl Gustav Jung (1875 – 1961) was completely convinced that dreams offered practical advice, sent from the unconscious to the conscious self. He felt passionately that such self-understanding would lead to a fuller and a more productive life. Indeed, the astonishing work *'Man and His Symbols'* owes its very existence to one of Jung's own dreams. In this dream, instead of sitting in his study and conversing with the eminent doctors and psychiatrists who frequently consulted him from all over the world, Jung saw himself standing in a public place and addressing a multitude of people who were listening and *understanding everything that he said.*

For Jung, this dream was nothing short of a grand awakening and two weeks later, he agreed to write the book that was completed just before his death. It would not be an over estimation to say that Jung, who ranked alongside Einstein and Freud as one of the great minds of the twentieth century, revolutionized the entire process of creative thought. He began a transition that has led us to a closer understanding of the twin worlds of imagination and energy.

Dreams are, as Jung discovered, the ultimate communication from the soul. But whereas dream interpretation sees dreams from the outside in, accepting dreams as messages from the soul is understanding them from the *inside out.* And that's a huge difference....

Through our dreams (as well as our reincarnations) we are given unique opportunities to receive spiritual guidance, which can, in turn, lead to significant personal changes. Eventually, we begin to treat others the way we like to be treated. We learn that our actions have a deep affect on our immediate environment and, ultimately, upon the universe we inhabit. Minor actions can frequently have significant repercussions.

This is the beginning of *the evolution of the human soul.* When we finally learn to become compassionate, to love others equally – without fear, anger or thoughts of hate – we attain Nirvana, the complete cessation of the state of suffering, the end of separateness and the ultimate goal of Buddhist practice. This is when reincarnation ends.

UNIVERSAL LAWS – THE GREAT AWAKENING

'We learn to endure the unendurable and to accomplish the impossible'.
UPASAKASHILA SUTRA

The laws that guide the creation of energy and give birth to the human frame also flow throughout the universe.

As energy beings, we move around this universe and are not only subject to its principles but are profoundly affected by them.

The *Four Basic Principles of Creation,* otherwise known as the Universal laws, expresses the very essence of God and of who we, as children of Eden, really are. In the Kabbalah, it is said that God revealed this sacred knowledge to Adam and Eve in a special book given to them by the angel Raziel, keeper of the secrets of God. With their fall from grace, this book was taken away from them by God, but later returned to Adam by the archangel Raphael. It is said that Adam studied this book for the rest of his life, bequeathing it to his son Seth and from him, through to Abraham. The book is still hidden today, though its secrets can be read by those select few who have been given the knowledge to 'read' it...

It is important at this stage to mention that universal laws do *not* govern – for there is no external consciousness that has decided that we must stick to these rules and regulations. Just as the laws of physics attempt to explain the nature of the universe, so these four tenets are in themselves more of a description of the nature of all things that exist.

Ancient Egyptian and Hebrew texts refer to the field of energy that radiates outwards through the human body from a specific point. The name of this field is *Mer-Ka-Ba.* In Egyptian this translates very roughly to: *Mer* meaning Light, *Ka* meaning Spirit and *Ba* for Body. The Light-Spirit-Body complex that surrounds each and every cell of the human body is the pattern that forms the Star of David – the affirmation of our connection to God.

It is through the *Mer-Ka-Ba* grid that we tune into the energy of the entire universe. And it is via our thoughts, feelings and emotions – our belief systems – that we can alter the bioelectrical charge within the cellular structure of the physical body.

Every cell within every life form is constantly restructuring and reshaping its biochemical circuitry to generate, sustain and gather higher frequencies and the complex array of radiant pranic energy.

Everything that you, as an individual, have ever felt, known, touched, created or thought generates a process in which you perceive the world around you and which, in turn, changes the way the world works – forever.

It makes great sense therefore to discover that the Four Principles with which we interact so intimately are: *Love, Health and Well Being, Abundance* and *Creativity.*

Love remains the greatest of the four principles.

It is intimately related to the way we think and without it, as the Dalai Lama reminds us, it is impossible to find happiness. This is the true measure of 'charity' that St. Paul speaks so passionately of, for it allows us to treat others the way we should like to be treated.

All things exist within this one law and are created out of it. *Love is the total and complete acceptance of what is. It allows. It breathes. It accepts.* Without love, free will could not exist.

The universe is a place of creation as well as a place of experience. Remember that you have come into this world by choice to experience yourself just as you have done in previous incarnations. Once you begin to realize that you are loved, dearly loved and accepted beyond all measure, you can then start to master the other universal laws and move closer to the Higher power of God.

We are bathed in positive electrical potential all our lives. Embedded in each and every one of us is something that can fittingly be described as an 'atom'. This atom holds within it, the will to love. A huge magnet to the greater expression of love, universal love and love of God, it is this 'atom' that draws us forward in our development, it is what propels you as an individual from one incarnation to another, until the cycle of love has been completed. Dickens's Ebenezer Scrooge, whose heart was ice, eventually thawed to the warmth of the open heart chakra and allowed love to flow abundantly from himself to other people in one of literature's most touching personal transformations. At the end of the novel, we are told that Scrooge's "own heart laughed" for joy as he grew in compassion with the world alongside of him.

Lack of love, on the other hand, is founded in seeing others around you as potential threats.

It is also refusing to become "involved" in other people's lives through the act of indifference. But, there is a price to be paid for such behavior.

According to the laws of karma, the very indifference you show to others will one day be the same indifference that you may encounter! So, be very careful before you adopt this attitude. Is this what you really want? If you decide consciously and deliberately to ignore the sufferings of your fellow man, you end up ultimately creating a world in which your suffering is also of no concern to others.

The person whose heart is closed to love or who has a distorted perception of love (as needs based rather than as giving) and who delights in making other people around him as miserable as he is, is destined to live in a world devoid of love. That is the nature of the universe.

By consistently refusing to open their hearts to the endless possibility of love, such people create their own loveless existence. There is much validity in Jean-Paul Sartre's statement that hell is other people. Sometimes, it is. But such people, whose lives are dominated by fear, anger and hatred, cannot actually 'kill' love because it really is the natural state of all sentient beings.

We are all born with the same potential. We all have the same capacity for compassion, the same power of thought – all that is needed is to engage, fully and absolutely, the glorious principle of the open heart of love because only love endures....

We fill our busy lives with activity but tend to give little if any thought to being still, to attaining peace of mind. *Health and Well Being* the second of the Four Principles, are also natural states of being. Good health is the birthright of each and every one of us.

From an energy perspective, illness and disease are primarily the result of negative thoughts and the resulting fears that they manifest block the flow of positive prana. Without a diet of love, gratitude and acceptance how can we ever heal?

In the children's classic *'The Wizard of Oz'* author Frank L. Baum touched the heart of this principle when Glinda, the Good Witch of the North, reminds Dorothy that she had the power to return to her home in Kansas all along.

Rebuked, Glinda remarks that Dorothy would not have believed her initially – she had to find this out for herself, whereupon the Scarecrow, with his brand new brain, is moved to blurt out that this truth is so simple he should have thought of it himself!

Baum, a Theosophist who championed a new world of human spirituality in which a higher truth endowed humans with almost limitless capacities, was in fact discussing the power we all possess – through the understanding that fears are just fears, not reality. When you can achieve this you will find that you are liberated from the paralyzing emotion of fear and you can free yourself from the original cause of illness and disease. You can, in fact, 'go home' as Dorothy Gale did.

For many of us though, the process of leaving fear behind can be easier said than done.

We live in a world that is quite literally built on fear. The insurance industry operates exclusively on this emotion; many a successful marketing campaign has been based on it and even some of the world's greatest religions have been underpinned by fear!

Since the September 11 tragedy, most Americans now live in what has been described as a 'culture of fear'. And other western nations have, as a consequence, enacted legislation that has even eroded precious personal freedoms! Some psychologists see fear as a useful emotion as it can warn against unpleasant situations or consequences, while others state categorically that fear is quite a redundant quality.

In direct contrast to western ideologies on fear, the Dharmic faiths in the East see fear as a form of karmic suffering from which we are challenged to grow spiritually.

To Buddhists fear is nothing but another form of attachment to our mortal life, our 'self' and all our material possessions.

With the attainment of the Third Nobel Truth – the cessation of suffering – the Buddha taught that everything that occurs in life (such as fear) could also cease. When we act to conquer our fears (by letting go of them and detaching from them), we are freed from fear. The way we do this is through the quality of compassion and honesty.

This is having faith and trusting in God.

The third of the Four Universal Principles is: *Abundance.*

This area has recently received massive public interest following the airing of the television documentary (and later book) called *'The Secret'.*

For the uninitiated *'The Secret'* talks about an ancient Law – The Law of Attraction – that works whether we are aware of it or not. This law states that what you think is what you get, and what you think is what you are.

Most people are convinced that life just somehow 'happens'

and that things impose themselves on you. Western culture and western society is anchored around this premise, whilst most indigenous cultures and eastern philosophies adhere to the complete opposite.

The Principle of *Abundance* states that part of your life's purpose is to move beyond lack, scarcity and limitation. Here we see the affirmation; "The Lord helps those who help themselves" in action.

Although the experience of 'lack' can be valuable in terms of learning certain lessons at certain times, *it is not required as a learning tool.*

As incredible as it may well seem to some people, poverty, lack and scarcity actually stem from mankind's most primal fear – that of being separated from The Source. The Source is, of course, yourself. Through an understanding of the miracle of universal energy – in which the Law of Attraction plays an undeniable part – we learn to use *our own* God-given powers to heal ourselves and others. Somehow, contemporary Western man has failed to strike a balance between the medieval ideal of wholly depending on God and the modern mantra of total reliance on the ego. *We have forgotten to affirm ourselves as essentially spiritual beings with creative powers – powers given to us by The Supreme Being.*

But it was not always so.

In the late 19th century, French pharmacist Emile Coue became fascinated by the power of the mind and began practicing "mind conditioning therapy" in his clinic. The well-known phrase: "Every day in every way, I'm getting better and better" came from Coue. What he had discovered was that effective affirmations affect outcomes. If repeated out loud or written down several times a day for weeks, these 'thought forms' manifest as reality.

What *'The Secret'* has done is to make many people aware of this simple energy transfer.

"The Law of Attraction states that everything draws to itself that which is like itself". As a being of light energy you are a magnet – everything that you have created, every last cell, every bodily contour, each nail and strand of hair is a total expression of who you are. It is an expression of your consciousness.

In a way, Karma too is an expression of the Law of Attraction but in this instance it is based on redemption and reincarnation. What you give is what you get.

Everything in your life and the lives of the people around you is affected by the Principle of Abundance.

Nothing in your life manifests by accident – it happens because you made it happen. *All energy follows thought.* As matter is energy, it too will follow thought. But it must be remembered that energy is neutral and is molded by your individual thoughts. Such energy can only, and will only be formed by what you are thinking.

So when you want to attract something into your life and you do nothing but think of *the lack of that thing,* the Universe will bring you exactly this – lack. Negative thoughts create negative happenings. When you feel poor, you do not attract prosperity. By thinking that you are rich *and by being grateful* for the money that you do have, you draw money to you. If you feel fat, you cannot attract thin. If you fear ill health, you will attract ill health. If you fear loneliness, you will attract loneliness.

That which you give thought to is that which you begin to invite into your experience. The Universe does not judge.

Unfortunately, just as most people have launched a new thought about what they want, within a few days they may begin to think of something different. Remember the universe responds instantly to you – if yesterday, you believed that you were going to meet the man of your dreams soon, but today you feel somewhat skeptical about this, then today this is what the Universe will bring you – nothing. This is the thought you put out. This is a cancellation of your original order!

When you surround yourself with your personal affirmations (a picture board, or notes hung around your home, on your computer etc.) you will begin to focus daily on these thoughts and you will see these changes begin to manifest in your life.

Heraclitus once wrote: "Day by day, what you choose, what you think and what you do is who you become...". I once knew a literary agent who was always bemoaning the fact that publishers consistently turned down the manuscripts she offered them. She would talk frequently about this distressing state of affairs in a sad and melancholy voice. Her attitude was one of weary resignation. Despite the fact that she was a lovely person with a very sweet nature, she attracted this energy into her life by daily manifesting these thoughts. This is the power of the Law of Attraction.

Well before he became a sought-after actor, Jim Carey ambitiously wrote himself a $10 million check for "acting services rendered" and years later made the news for being signed for just this amount!

Even the Bible urges us to think positive thoughts. Jesus said: "Ask and ye shall receive". In Philippians 4:8 we are advised to pay attention to: "whatever is true, whatever is noble, whatever is right, whatever is pure, whatever is lovely, whatever is admirable – if anything is excellent or praiseworthy – think about such things".

We are unique, valuable and precious expressions of God. As you arrive at a greater state of 'having', you will receive more of this experience until you create abundance in every single area of your life.

The final Principle of the Universe is *Creativity.*

This law lies at the nucleus of every soul and every person.

We are, quite simply, driven to create our own experiences. As you begin this process of creation, you will discover more about who you really are. It is the fundamental nature of the soul to be creative. The ways we express ourselves though are not necessarily limited to the roles we occupy in life or the jobs we fill.

Being creative is about living a life that is filled with love, experiencing the joy of health and well being, feeling abundant in every single aspect of life and *being able to create all of these experiences freely.*

Your soul's purpose was to manifest itself through you in harmony with these Four Universal Laws.

By appreciating the gifts that have been given by God, by allowing ourselves to live lives filled with love and compassion, by being grateful and, above all, through the power of forgiveness, we resonate with positive prana. We alter the frequency of our field of magnetic attraction and we help to change the world around us – forever. We become the "Power of Now" that Eckhart Tolle talks so powerfully about. We can heal the incurable. We can become 'whole'.

In Jewish tradition it is frequently said that "the most beautiful thing a man can do is to forgive wrong". Whenever in life we encounter raw pain, anguish or suffering it can be all too easy to fall into the pit of despair. The Christian ethic of forgiveness, the lesson of the Cross, is in hard cold reality such a difficult lesson to master. Yet, master it we must. In Buddhist philosophy and teachings, enemies are seen as precious because it is through them that we are challenged to grow. Even the word 'forgive' is interesting as it is derived from the old English verb *gifan* meaning, quite literally, 'to give'. When we forgive others, we 'give up' and release these negative emotions and memories to the universe. Our energy field stops shrinking and shines in brilliancy as we grow closer to God...

Beyond the astral plane, there exist many other planes of light energy and it is in these planes that your soul, as incredible as it may sound, has existed forever. In these astonishing realms of Divine light you actually discovered and learnt with the special creative 'abilities' that have always flourished there. Through this experience, you have already learnt to know yourself on the spiritual level – all that remains is to attain this enlightenment on the physical plane. This is now your mission, should you choose to accept it….

ANGELS & DEMONS – THE POWER OF GOODNESS & THE PRESENCE OF EVIL

"And I saw the seven angels which stood before God."
Revelation 8:2

Helping us to achieve this state of one-ness by directing and assisting the flow of universal energy on the physical plane are our guides – angels.

But, before any discussion on angels and the essential role they play within the human energy matrix takes place, we must first probe the nature of **positive and negative energies** that operate so powerfully both in our lives and in our world.

Nothing – absolutely nothing – can be manifested in a finite world without its opposite. Just as there are positive neutrons, so too are there negative neutrons. Light implies darkness, or else it would not be known as light, and as for breathing, this act simply could not be sustained unless we breathed *both in and out.*

The Beriatric Tree of Life, so beloved of Kabbalists, depicts the forces and forms that co-exist on either branches born of the momentum of creation. These twin cosmic pillars represent good and evil and are constantly in motion pushing and pulling, expanding and contracting. This separation of Light from Darkness, Heaven from Hell, consciousness from unconsciousness are all part and parcel of the harmony of the spheres put into place by God at Creation.

Like Heaven, Hell has its own hierarchy described by Jesus as the 'bent back' with its levels of senior demons (fallen angels) and lesser demons or subordinates. Sometimes, during exorcisms, an evil spirit will say that he wants to leave the possessed person but cannot as "he" won't let me – the "he" referring either to his immediate superior or the Devil, himself.

I am often asked about both the role and the problem of evil energies and my answer is the same: like the double action of the human heart, the heartbeat of the universe implies duality – a sort of cosmic pulse, an alteration of breathing in and of breathing out.

Evil exists.

Yet its existence is not some kind of Divine examination that we either pass or fail. Nor is it "sent to test us", as we so often find ourselves saying. Evil exists because of man's inordinate desires for self – chiefly self-gratification. The three inner poisons of anger, lust and delusion, as well as karmic veils and obstructions that have been built up through many lifetimes sign post the road to evil. Most religious texts remind us forcibly of this. At the core of Buddhist teaching or dharma, all action directed to selfish, separate ends is fundamentally evil. All action, which tends to union, is good. Christian ethics are entrenched in love of neighbor and forgiveness, while in Judaism it is said that the greatest thing a man can ever do is to forgive evil...

There are basically two types of evil – conscious and unconscious. The first agent is usually demonic and knows exactly what he is doing as he pushes against the established order of the universe, while the second tempter is often a human being who indulges in evil for self gratification or who strays onto the left-hand path unintentionally and having got there, stays there, quite often deluding themselves. Both are toxic, the first more so than the second.

We know that evil demonstrates itself through behavior that troubles us yet we still tend, as a society, to think of evil almost as a physical entity – a knife, a gun etc. Our western culture portrays evil as a little red-skinned satanic creature with two horns, holding a pitchfork and wearing a spiked tail. The traditional belief is that this mythological and somewhat comical character compels us to destructive behavior. The reality is, as usual, quite different.

Satan was one of the most beautiful angels that God ever created and the children of Satan are often physically beautiful too. Satan, whose name means accuser/adversary/slanderer also has a host of other names. He is known alternatively as Lucifer (the 'light bearer'), Baal (the chief pagan god of the Canaanites), Belial, the Serpent, the Dragon, Abaddon (the 'destroyer'), the ruler of this world, even the prince of the power of the air.

The church of Satan, which was established in San Francisco in 1966, calls on its followers to "indulge" instead of abstaining, to seek "vengeance as opposed to turning the other cheek" and to "represent all the so-called sins as they lead to physical, mental or emotional gratification"! Official recognition of its members is now occurring around the world.

In October 2004, the BBC reported that the British armed forces had officially recognized its first registered Satanist – a move that meant that naval technician, Chris Cranmer, was now permitted to perform satanic rituals on board ship. A spokesperson for the Royal Navy responded: "We are an equal opportunities employer and we don't stop anybody from having their own religious values". (4)

As traditional religious values decline, evil ascends and today, unfortunately, evil (especially in the guise of a 'search for spirituality') is flourishing. As a light energy worker I find it truly disturbing to read reports like the BBC one above. Dark forces spend a great deal of time and effort to ensure that most people do not believe that they exist at all! BUT, I can assure you, they do.

The opposite of evil is, of course, love.

The finest qualities that mankind possesses (strength of purpose, patience, love, humility and unselfishness) have been gradually developed from the interplay between these twin energy forces. If a man, of his own free will, uses power for good, his gain will be proportionate.

If he opts to use power for evil, he is essentially pitting himself against the whole force of the universe. For a while he may seem to flourish in his transgression, but as is the nature of the universe, the karmic pendulum will bring him *dukkha,* the suffering that his acts have caused. His evil acts, in this instance, are as the thirteenth century philosopher and teacher Thomas Aquinas (1224/5 – 1274) so forcibly reminds us, a 'privation' for he has ultimately deprived himself of the equal opportunity to do good.

Angels are the unseen hands, which guide us on the path of goodness, the messengers from God, the source of all energy. As Saint Francis de Sales advised: "Make yourself familiar with the angels, and behold them frequently in spirit; for without being seen, they are present with you".

We are reminded by St. Augustine that: "every visible thing in this world is put under the charge of an angel". This is something that we should never forget.

In addition to guardian angels, there are hundreds of named angels for given situations and from whom we can seek help. The ancient religious sect, The Essenes, who lived around two thousand years ago on the shores of the Dead Sea were skilled in healing and angelology (the study of angels). They believed that by communing daily with angels, physical and spiritual well being could be achieved. Although they were but a single link in a secret chain of ancient wisdom, the Essenes are thought to have written most (if not all) of the Dead Sea Scrolls in which the names of many angels and the parts they play in transforming the lives of humans are written.

In 1993, *Time Magazine* conducted a rather unusual survey of the American people called: 'Angels Among Us'. In it, a staggering 69 per cent of those polled believe that angels exist and have an effect on people's lives – with one in three people openly admitting that they had had an 'angelic encounter'. (5)

According to the world's major religions angels are definitely real and not the figment of some medieval imagination.

In the Old Testament Angels appeared in a dream to Isaac's son, Jacob, in human form devoid of wings and climbing a ladder between heaven and earth. In Islamic tradition, the prophet Mohammed received the words of the Koran from the angel Gabriel (known as Jibral), the spirit of truth, and believed that nothing could occur without the presence of angels. In Christianity, angels have been present since creation.

The profession of faith of the Fourth Lateran Council of the Church of Rome in 1215 affirms that God "from the beginning of time made at once (simul) out of nothing both orders of creatures, the spiritual and the corporeal – that is, the angelic and the earthly, and then (deinde) the human creature, who as it were shares in both orders, being composed of spirit and body".

For Aquinas, who became known as the 'Angel Doctor', each angel was the sole member of its species – 'all intellect' and without matter. Emanuel Swedenborg, the eighteenth century Swedish theologian and scientist, was so obsessed with angels that he spent the last 25 years of his life delving into angelic experiences and theories and concluded that as humans we see angels through the soul. He called this 'portal' an inward eye that was directly reflective of an individual's ability to receive goodness and truth. Although he clearly had no idea what he had stumbled upon, Swedenborg could just as easily have been talking about the Third Eye Chakra, which is our connection to the Supreme Being.

In the Middle Ages, angelology assumed such an importance in the daily lives of ordinary people that farming activities, days of the week, animals and plants, even astrological signs were all subject to their own angelic influences. Angelology was very much the European Feng Shui.

It is important to note that angels differ significantly from spirits or ghosts.

In almost every single case that I have researched and personally come across, the earthbound or trapped spirits of the dead are reported as being chill entities that are transparent and free-floating. Ghosts retain their earthly shells as well as their personalities and many can be contacted through mediums with messages that are either welcome or unwelcome.

Angel encounters on the other hand are always distinguishable by their positive energy – there are numerous case studies where people have described angels as 'luminous', warm beings who exude a tremendous sense of calm. We all have angels around us *constantly and without exception* and these beings are eager and excited about the opportunity to communicate with us.

The main task of an angel is *to bear witness to the truth.*

The 'Truth' here is that God is *with us and for us*. As beings of energy, this powerful message can be either a warning to us or a comfort to us in times of danger or transformation.

In their protective roles, angels can be the fiercest of warriors and the swiftest of rescuers. When God passes justice on injustice, angels are often the ones who carry out the sentence. Jesus speaks of children as having their own angels, while the angel Gabriel told Mohammed that God is veiled by 70,000 veils of light and darkness and that God communicates to mortals through the angelic hierarchy. As for Satan, Revelation tells us that at the end of the world, God will simply send an angel from Heaven with a large chain to bind up the Devil and thrust him into the "lake of fire and sulphur" where his torment will last "day and night for ever and ever". Hell, no less.

Angels remain our helpers in responding to the Truth and they guide us, sometimes calling us to take a specific action. They do not negotiate – unless God tells them to. Nor do they decay or die, as they are essentially spiritual beings. They even pray for us and are among the unseen in "all that is seen and unseen" of the Christian Nicene Creed. They exist to praise God and to bear the message and task for which God sends them. *They appear to all people of all religions, or even of no religion at all, when God wants these people to listen.*

Seeing Angels

There have been times in my life when I have been overcome by total pain or despair and I have been so busy just trying to grapple with the enormity of what was happening to me, that I failed to notice the tiny spiritual space that had opened up and allowed a small wave of positive angelic energy to flow in.

But this is what happens when angels manifest in your life. The 'dark night of the soul', as described by the great Spanish mystic St. John of the Cross, is frequently illuminated by the presence of angels.

My first personal encounter with angelic beings was extraordinary and I have come to believe passionately that angels function in similar ways to spirit guides, though their powers are quite different.

For many years, as I mentioned earlier, I had grappled with a very dark energy force that had manifested in a malicious and drawn-out psychic war between light and dark forces. At a particularly low moment during this exhausting struggle, I was hanging out the family washing one morning when I was filled with a tremendous feeling of peace and serenity. To this day, I don't know what compelled me to look up into the tall gum trees that surround the house. But I did. What I saw amazed even me.

Three luminous translucent and very tall beings were sitting calmly in the branches of the nearest tree, just looking at me. For what seemed like an eternity, we gazed at one another, then the golden beings looked away into the sky. I followed their gaze (it seemed the most natural thing for me to do) and saw the sky become filled with dark objects that were travelling like a swarm of angry bees at lightning speed in my direction. These angelic beings did not flinch but continued to focus intently on the black objects. As these negative energy forms approached, they were repelled as if an invisible hand had simply pushed them gently but firmly away and they were returned in a neat black spiral to the sender.

With the sky clear once more, the beings then turned their gaze back to me and I was filled with an extraordinary sense of tranquility and gratitude. It was at that moment that I knew that I was loved, that our *only* purpose as human beings is to love and be loved. I felt very humbled. For the rest of that day, these three angelic beings sat in the tree. The next morning, they were gone...

Eileen Elias Freeman is the director of the AngelWatch Foundation, a non-profit organization that serves as a major resource centre on the topic of angels. The author of many books on angels and holder of a master's degree in Theology, Freeman's life has been touched by angels since she was five years old. Her personal experiences are quite simply amazing, but for me the most poignant remains that of a hospital visit by an angel to her while she was waiting to undergo surgery. Freeman had suffered a violent reaction to an antibiotic when she was visited by an angel who embraced her with light, warmth and peace. Within an hour, she began to heal to the incredulity of her doctors. Following this experience she wrote the electrifying book: *'Angelic Healing: Working with Your Angels to heal Your Life'.* (6)

Hospitals are places that literally teem with angels. There are numerous reports of visitations being made to people on their sickbed by the Angel of Death. Those enduring long or painful illness, even those who keep vigil beside the beds of the sick have witnessed the comforting presence of angels. Many nurses and doctors tell me that they hear stories of angelic presences all the time although some attribute these experiences to the effects of drug therapy!

The Mothman Prophecies

Between November 1966 and December 1967, the sleepy little town of Point Pleasant, West Virginia in the US, became gripped by visitations from a "dark terror" that culminated in a tragedy that made headlines all over the world.

For thirteen months homes throughout the region were plagued with unearthly noises, ghostly manifestations and electrical interference, while mysterious glowing lights travelled across the night sky on a regular basis. The population soon became terrified as apparitions of winged "monsters" soared along darkened highways, appeared in farmsteads and followed cars at night. Dubbed "The Mothman" by the press, eyewitness accounts describe this being as a "big, grey thing…bigger than a man…with terrible, glowing red eyes". All reported feeling an uncontrollable and indescribable terror.

As the Christmas season approached, visits by the Mothman intensified across the Point Pleasant area and on the day of the collapse of the Silver Bridge, connecting West Virginia with Ohio, the Mothman continued to appear.

Many people lost their lives that day but residents now believe that the Mothman was actually trying to warn them about the forthcoming disaster.

One account told of how the Mothman had hovered outside the bedroom window of a young girl on the eve of the disaster. The girl and her family were scheduled to leave on a trip the next day and their route would have taken them over the bridge. As they pulled out of their driveway though, the child's father had a sudden crippling headache and felt so sick that he had to go back inside the house to lie down for a while. When he recovered a short time later, he turned on the radio to hear of the disaster his family had so narrowly avoided.

Later investigations revealed that this same being had been seen in Chernobyl, Russia by many of the local people prior to the nuclear disaster of 1986. His presence undeniably foretells a chain of tragic events. Wherever the Mothman appears death soon follows...

When I first came across this story I was fascinated by the descriptions people gave of the Mothman because they bear a remarkable resemblance to the Angel of Death.

Created by God on the first day of creation, the Angel of Death is said to have 12 enormous wings (the Mothman was reputed to have wingspan of more than ten feet wide) and to be "full of eyes" (witnesses reported that the Mothman had large, red glowing and hypnotic eyes).

While angels come in all shapes and sizes, Archangels are universally TALL (the Mothman was said to have been over 7 feet in height).

The Bible takes great trouble to tell us that the Angel of Death is *not* evil, nor is he a fallen angel. He remains at all times a legate of God and in God's service.

It would therefore come as no surprise to discover that his presence would engender electrical interference – as a highly evolved energy being, electrical disturbances would be a natural consequence of his presence in the region. And, although there were reports of animals being mutilated in the Point Pleasant area, the incidents were more likely to be the result of human activity – and that strictly of the black magic kind whose members use these mutilation techniques in a foolish and futile bid to harness an energy force they know very little about!

Whatever people chose to believe, the presence of the Mothman heralds a disaster where the loss of human life is great. His presence and his message should, I believe, be taken seriously and with great respect. He comes to prepare us for death....

Nasa, Feathers and Fragrance

Over the years it has not been unusual for NASA astronauts to report angelic encounters. One individual claimed that an angel clearly hovered above him on a spacewalk, while others have sighted angels in orbit flying outside the windows of the spaceship itself. Some airline pilots frantic with worry and facing the trauma of difficult landings have also reported angelic sightings. In one instance, cockpit recordings revealed the tremendous sense of calm that came over a crew as they successfully averted a crash. On the tape, the men talk of an unidentified object flying alongside the plane, with the pilot describing an angel flitting outside the plane's front window. (7)

Some of the signs of an angelic encounter are the sensation of being enveloped by a pair of large, fluffy wings, of seeing either a huge glowing human like figure, or that of a small child with golden hair. Others include finding a tiny white feather, a powerful feeling of warmth and comfort, the appearance of a bright light or color within the mind, a tingling in the air or on the hands, and even the smell of a sudden fragrance. In the latter instance, many people describe a floral perfume – often like nothing the person has ever smelt before or since – though this fragrance can also be a scent that the person has been familiar with in the past.

Melanie was a single mother with two young children who had just such an experience many years ago.

One morning, while driving to work, she came out of the main highway to find herself directly in the path of an oncoming truck that was accelerating rapidly towards her. When she noticed the truck, she flew into a panic, as she knew that she was going to be hit. At that moment, all she could think about was her two small children and, momentarily, she closed her eyes and prayed. At that precise moment, the truck brushed past her, missing her car by centimeters. Although she was badly shaken, she kept going. Within seconds, the most exquisite floral scent filled the car and Melanie began to calm down. To her this was an extraordinary happening, as it was the dead of winter, she had chosen not to wear any perfume that morning and her car windows were all closed.

Bad Angels

Just as there are good angels, so too are there bad ones.

No exploration on the energy dynamics of these beings would be complete without mention of this significant fact.

Unlike angels, demons (fallen angels) have no message of their own to tell – only lies, so that they undermine God's message. Since they have been deprived of their natural purpose, the demons' very existence is twisted up and broken. Satan is generally depicted as peer to the archangels Michael and Gabriel and it has been written that Satan can even come disguised as an angel of light. It is not unusual for demons to disguise themselves as celestial beings – but unlike the real thing, they are conspicuous by the fact that they sew the seeds of doubt about the true essence of God. These spirits of fire and air are adroit at puffing up the ego, at manipulating and directing, demanding attention and eventually reshaping the unfortunate human into their image.

A few years ago, I came across a book on angels that had been written by a lady who claimed to be guided by a spirit. As I worked my way through the chapters, all the signs of demonic presence were so evident (game-playing, emotional blackmail, egocentrism etc.) that I was left feeling very uneasy. This individual clearly had no idea (neither did her publishers) of how she had been duped. I can only repeat: good angels do *not* play games. They do not try to run your life....

For a comprehensive history of the Fall of Angels, we must look at the **Book of Enoch.**

This remarkable lost book of the Bible was first discovered in a monastery in Abyssinia (now Ethiopia) in 1773 by a Scottish explorer named James Bruce. Further investigation revealed that the ancient text had been written in the second or first century BC in Hebrew or Aramaic, and later translated into Greek, Ethiopic and Latin. In 1821, Dr. Richard Lawrence, Archbishop of Cashel and a Hebrew Professor at Oxford, translated the book into English.

In modern times, more recent discoveries of copies of the book were found among the Dead Sea Scrolls at Qumran and prove beyond doubt that the Enoch testament was in existence well before the time of Jesus. In fact it is entirely possible that Christ himself studied the text as over one hundred phrases in the New Testament can be traced back to the Enoch scrolls.

Although it had once been an integral part of the Bible and Jewish teachings, the Book of Enoch the Prophet disappeared from the religious world quite simply because it fell into disfavor with powerful theologians at some time during the 4th century BC.

Its controversial statements on the nature and deeds of evil angels were considered unsuitable for public consumption. In the Old Testament, these fallen angels are referred to as "sons of God', but this has now been accepted as a mistranslation and actually should read "angels of God". Unfortunately, this error has led to many misunderstandings. Yet, in spite of being denunciated as heresy, cursed, and banned by Church leaders, with almost uncanny persistence the Book of Enoch eventually found its way back into circulation and the story it had to tell was, quite literally, explosive....

The Biblical figure Enoch was the son of Cain. He is reputed to have lived 365 years and is said to have enjoyed a close relationship with God. The intimacy of this relationship resulted in Enoch's being transported to Heaven (Genesis 5:24), where he was shown the secrets of the universe and of all time.

It is somehow eminently fitting that Enoch was to become the author of a work that describes in detail the workings of the universe and God's ultimate plan to save the righteous and punish the wicked, for the Book of Enoch is ripe with imageries of light and dark energies and the forces that cloak the universe. It is an incredible work, breath-taking in its simplicity and its prophecies for the fate of mankind. It is the testament of a visionary.

In his writings, Enoch records the fall of about 200 angels (he names about 19 of them) whom he calls the *Fallen Ones* or *The Watchers*.

Religious leaders and theologians have poured over the Enoch manuscripts and taking into account other earlier texts have come to the conclusion that there were in fact two distinct celestial falls – that of Satan leading a third of the angelic host in open rebellion against God and that of the *Grigori* (or Watchers).

According to Enoch, Satan was at first a good angel created by God who, in company with other angels, "became evil by their own doings". Through misuse of the gifts of intellect, Satan declared himself as great as God and led a rebellion of angels against the celestial order. In Revelation 12, verse 7, we are told that: "War broke out in Heaven" when Satan refused to pay homage to a creature of clay (Adam) .The Archangel Michael and his angels arose for God and fought the dragon (Satan) and his legions. Defeated, the Devil and his followers were tossed out of Heaven and hurled down to the earth. Here, they have subsequently continued to wage war against God by attempting to ruin God's creation, man. Their offspring took a physical incarnation and were known as the *Nephilim* (the "cast down ones"). Satan, himself, became known as "the prince of this world" and Jesus tells us that God extinguished Satan's spiritual light and that the Devil took the face of a man.

The second angelic fall concerns the *Grigori*.

These are the angels who lusted after the beautiful daughters of men, and came down to earth to mate with them. This mysterious eighth order of angels was originally created by God to be the earthy shepherds of the first humans.

The Grigori were said to be both physically and spiritually gigantic. When they, of their own will, defied God and mated with humans they bred *Demons* called *Gibborim* - giants of extraordinary power and intellect. They are referred to in Genesis as "heroes of old" and "men of renown".

This interference by the Fallen Angels is widely regarded as the birth of evil in the world and Enoch is entrusted through a series of vivid visions to intercede with them and to warn them of their final, horrible fate.

In the manuscripts, Enoch relates how he is taken by various angelic light beings throughout the realms of earth and hell (Sheol), through to the "pillars of Heaven", to the place of final judgment for the fallen ones and to the Garden of Righteousness that has been set aside for the good. The imagery and symbolism of these passages is reminiscent of Revelation with its exquisite poetry and continual references to light energy.

The gigantic offspring of the fallen angels were endowed, Enoch tells us, with the knowledge of how to manufacture deadly weapons with which to wage war on mankind, they were skilled in the making of mirrors, jewellery, cosmetics and dyes and received lessons in sorcery, astrology, divination and astronomy from the fallen angels.

That giants stalked the earth at this moment in time is hard historical fact. Records reveal that Og, the King of Bashan, had a bed that was 13 to 15 feet long, while the Philistine warrior Goliath was six cubits tall (about nine feet). These Gibborim also had six fingers and six toes. (Today, these are routinely removed shortly after birth.)

Enoch also says that these demons freely injured all animal and bird life that roamed the earth eating their flesh and drinking their blood and he refers to them as 'biters'.

There is no doubt in my mind that it is here where we see the emergence of the Vampire on earth.

As these demonic creations turned on the rest of mankind, Enoch says that humans "cried out and their voice reached to Heaven". God answered their cries for help and sent the Archangels Michael, Gabriel, Raphael, Suryal and Uriel to destroy the Nephilim and Gibborim host in a flood, chain up the Watchers and thus restore life to the earth…

Many ancient and contemporary writers have hypothesized that the mythical city of Atlantis was the original seat of demonic power on earth. Personally, I find no reason to dispute this especially as the Greek philosopher Plato takes pains to remind us that the Atlanteans were a highly technically advanced race (they were supposed to have had the first computers known to man) – but that they were a proud and haughty people (noted Satanic traits). Following the destruction of Atlantis "in one day and night of disaster" by "violent earthquakes and floods", survivors were scattered to the far corners of the earth where, it is said, they continue to plague mankind.

If the Enoch text is taken seriously (as I believe it should be) then it is also highly possible that the ancient gods and goddesses of Greek and Roman mythology may well have been none other than the Watchers themselves in a bid to control and dominate human affairs.

With their Fall, the Watchers lost the ability to communicate with God and any memories that they possessed of their former lives in service to the Divine Being, were erased. Their energies also fell and they began to grow denser, vibrating to lower inner earth frequencies. Their ability to tolerate light, warmth and love shrank. With no hope of salvation and nothing to lose, their aim has been to destroy mankind.

It is often reported in many texts that Satan and his demonic followers have 'dominion' over the first and second realms (earth and outer space). But this, in my opinion, is another error. It is more likely, if one takes into account the energetic readings that one gets when working on individuals with demonic possessions, that *these are the only spheres within which such low energy can actually vibrate.* Once an 'infected' or possessed person lifts his/her energy field to a higher frequency, dark energy loses its grip and falls rapidly away.

From the perspective of universal energy, the Book of Enoch makes profound sense. It is a rare and important record of the ascent of man and the birth of evil in the world.

In 1976, prominent Catholic scholar J.T. Milik wrote: *'The Books of Enoch: Aramaic Fragments of Qumran Cave 4'* (8). This 400-page work was a complete history of the Enochian writings. Milik's opinions, based as they are on years of in-depth research, continue to be highly respected. He was left in no doubt as to the authenticity of the 'Book of Enoch the Prophet'. Neither should we be.

Tree of Angels

According to Aquinas (and later illustrated exquisitely by the Qabalist Monks in their Tree of the Angelic World), Angels can be divided up into nine orders known as 'choirs'. These choirs are subsequently split into three groups of three referred to as 'Triads'.

The **first triad** and highest level of celestial beings comprise *Seraphim, Cherubim and Thrones. Seraphim* are top-ranking angels and live closest to the Throne of God. In Isaiah 6:2, they are described as having four faces, six glowing red wings and as carrying swords of flaming red, the Fires of Love. In direct communication with God, the Seraphim chant continuously: 'Holy, Holy, Holy' which resonates at high frequencies. This chant is said to hold the tension for the vibration of pure love throughout the universe and the frequency of the creation of all life, as we know it.

Cherubim hold the knowledge of God and are the keepers of all wisdom. These warrior angels, clothed in the deepest blue, guard the way to the Tree of Life at the East Gate of Eden, where God placed them. Frequently sent to earth to perform special divine tasks, the Cherubim are mighty guardians armed with swords that are ever turning. Their mission is to seek out and destroy demons.

Thrones are the dispensers of God's judgment. They are both the 'message' and the 'messenger' that Jacob's vision discloses.

Also known as Ophanim, these angels are described as looking like great wheels covered with eyes and glowing with light. They act with impartiality and humility and are said to lie at the beginning of the ladder from Heaven to earth.

Thus the first Triad is pure energy sometimes transposing into matter before reverting back to energy once more. They represent the Divine energy of love, light and, as a consequence, life itself.

The **second triad** is the least known of all the angelic hierarchies but remains one of crucial importance - for this level of angelic beings holds the delicate balance between those nearest to God (the first triad) and those nearest to mankind (the third triad). It comprises *Dominions, Virtues and Powers.*

Known as the Hashmallin, the *Dominions* receive their orders from the Seraphim and Cherubim and are responsible for ensuring the stability of the cosmos. They are also called the 'Regulators' or 'Channels of Mercy' and are often illustrated as holding a staff in one hand and a seal in the other. Christians singing praises to the 'Lord of Lords' refer to the Dominions. The Hashmallin guard the secret name of God.

Virtues are intimately connected with the on-going spiritual struggle for good over evil. These are the miracle workers of the angelic world and psychics or seers able to raise their spiritual consciousness can connect with this level of spiritual beings. These angels grant the courage and compassion to perform great deeds. Virtues are thus deeply concerned with the natural world.

Powers are the keepers of human souls. They act as an elite guard patrolling the boundary between Heaven and earth. Their main tasks are to make sure that no evil enters the Kingdom of Heaven and to ensure the safe passage of souls from the mortal world to the next. It is here, in this sixth choir, that the greatest risk of corruption lies and it is from here that Enoch the prophet records the demise of those beings who became the' fallen angels'.

The duty of a Powers angel is to restrain the power of demons, ensuring that they do not harm others.

The **third triad** comprises *Principalities, Archangels and Angels.* This is the choir that forms the army of God carrying guidance from the first and second triads, and dispensing heavenly blessings on earth.

The *Principalities* look after and monitor the human world, guiding and protecting nations, cities and towns.

Archangels are God's messengers and carry Divine Decrees from the Principalities. Revelations describes seven angels as standing before God and these are widely accepted as being Archangels. Christian and Jewish faiths agree on the number seven (but cannot agree on who the actual seven are – seven being a mystic number), while the Koran mentions four Archangels, but names only two – Michael and Gabriel. The chief task of Archangels is to shepherd mankind on earth.

Angels are the humble foot soldiers of the celestial choirs. The most popular of course, being the Guardian Angel. However all angels at this level keep watch over human souls and help to protect them from evil.

When people – especially other healers and psychics, talk about 'guides' and 'helpers', they can of course be referring to other souls who have crossed over, but I speak from personal experience when I say that angels are often guides as well and they can in fact take any form that is needed to help those of us in times of crisis. They may even 'talk' to us through others.

The message that angels bring to us in times of great change, tragedy or sickness is one of enduring love and the knowledge that, as beings of light energy, we are destined to exist in a sphere of love – love that can sometimes come disguised as a gift of pain. The Zohar, reminds us that there are palaces whose gates open only to tears. "In the desert of the heart," the text goes, "let the healing fountain start". Often when we are in the midst of great suffering in this life, we can see, hear and feel the touch of an angel in many surprising ways.

Open your heart to an angel today, your life will never be the same again, I promise you....

Harry Potter and The Dark Side

In November, 2001, sixty Seventh Day Adventist schools throughout Australia made international news when they universally and completely banned Harry Potter books from all of their classrooms, over concerns that these works might encourage children to experiment with the occult. At the time John Hammond, Seven Day Adventist education director in Australia said that the books failed "to meet our school criteria" and added that the schools had a library policy that: "excludes any book acquisition about the occult or which could encourage children into the occult". (9)

An Adventist college in Nunawading, Melbourne, held parents information evenings during which they described the Potter books as "tools of the devil".

This has not been the first time that the globally popular books have been criticized and earlier that same year a British teacher's leader warned fans about the risks of "dabbling" in the darker side of the occult.

Author Rowling hit back at the complaints stressing that, on the contrary, the books were "very moral" in their representations of the struggle between good and evil.

So, who is right?

When viewed from the perspective of a rollicking good read, there is no doubt in my mind that the Potter books are exactly that – a good read. There are elements of fantasy and sheer escapism in the works that appeal to children and adults alike. But *it must not be forgotten that the entire storyline is set in a deep occult context.* There are numerous references to dark occult practices with the hero, Harry, an emerging wizard/sorcerer keen to learn how to harness his powers through the occult. Evil, in the Potter books is strongly identified with a selfish search for power and influence over others. It is portrayed as highly attractive to some, but the author also makes it clear that others who possess occultist skills choose to use their powers only for good. Dumbledore, the headmaster of Hogwarts school, is portrayed as a compassionate and gentle character, for example. Much has also been made of Rowling's rise from poverty to riches, of her writing the book on scraps of paper at a café in Edinburgh while on welfare payments. All of this makes it sound to the uninformed as if the author's fame has been somewhat 'magical' too – instead of the sheer hard work over many years that it took for her to find a suitable publisher!

Nevertheless, it is quite clear to me that Rowling has researched her subject well – from her works, it can be seen that she has a thorough and accurate knowledge of alchemy, charms, scrying, incantations, rituals, hand and thought magic and many other occult concepts – some of them from white magic but most, it must be admitted, from very dark magic indeed. It is therefore only reasonable to assume that Rowling has done some research at the very least and or, at worst, has had exposure to occultist practices. This, of course, is strictly her own affair – *but what concerns me greatly is that the Potter books provide ideas and in some cases actual spells that present the occult to children as a tool of empowerment. The occult – the dark side of the occult – is not a tool to be given to children or unsuspecting adults for that matter. When placed in the hands and minds of uninitiated and innocent humans it can desensitize, popularize and even feed negative energy in a major way.*

Unlike another former author on the occult, Dennis Wheatley, whose eight novels on black magic during the 1960s and '70s, also had phenomenal success, Rowling has placed no warnings on the inside of her books to alert readers to the dangers of dabbling in the occult.

On the fly-leaf Wheatley's first novel *The Devil Rides Out*, (1934), he cautioned: "I desire to state that I personally have never assisted at, or participated in, any ceremony connected with magic – black or white. Should any of my readers incline to a serious study of the subject, and thus come into contact with a man or a woman of Power, I feel that it is only right to urge them, most strongly, to refrain from being drawn into the practice of the Secret Art…to do so would bring them into dangers of a very real and concrete nature".

Wheatley, whose book was acclaimed by the critics as the finest work of black magic since Bram Stoker's *Dracula,* believed strongly in the existence of evil powers that could wreck both physical and mental havoc.

Personally, I find that the Potter books are *not* in the same league as Wheatley's or with their very evident struggles of good over the forces of evil. In the Potter books the idea of using sorcery to fight evil is a major component of the plot, anyone opposed to witchcraft or wizardry is mocked and painted as stupid.

We do not live in a world where witches and wizards openly dress in black robes with pointed hats (except at Halloween, an even more disturbing 'feast', as we shall shortly learn), we live in a world where *ordinary people seriously practice witchcraft, sorcery, spells and other occult methods to empower themselves and to deliberately harm others.*

Any books that popularize the dark arts to children of an impressionable age without a warning gives these works, in my opinion, even more sinister power. The golden rule must be: do not try to harness powers from the occult, do not call down spirits or summon the dead, do not point a wand, stick or even a ruler at anyone in a malevolent way. The occult is not a game and if ever you feel as if you are becoming obsessed with 'magic' to the exclusion of all else, this is the time to stop and seek help from a professional healer or a sanctified exorcist. Psychic powers, like all gifts, are neither good nor evil – but these energies can be used in a positive or a negative way. I have known of some very gifted psychics and healers who have been driven insane by forces they have unleashed and subsequently sought to control. We are not here to control spirits, pit demons against enemies or manipulate energetic forces. The unspoken law amongst all well-intentioned energy workers must remain: help any, but harm none.

Exorcism and Spirit Possession

It is an uncomfortable, but true fact, that spirit possession does happen. The Roman Catholic Church takes possession in modern life so seriously that in 1999, the Vatican issued its first new guidelines since 1614 on the driving out of devils, or exorcism, as it is more popularly called. (10)

In February 2005 about 100 Catholic priests signed up for the Vatican course on exorcism thus swelling the number of official exorcists in Italy to nearly 400, according to Church officials. But it seems that even these impressive numbers are not enough to handle the continuing avalanche of requests for help from hundreds of tormented people throughout Europe who believe that they are possessed. In the US, the shortage of official exorcists is even more acute.

So, what is going on?

We don't have to go too far to find out.

In today's climate of religious disarray, the ascendency of the spirituality revolution has inevitably opened the doors to some very negative and downright nasty energy forces as well as positive ones. In many ways, it has provided a public platform for groups that harness the powers of demonic entities to pass themselves off as a natural part of the world we all share. Nothing could be further from the truth....

There is no doubt in my mind that we are in the midst of a major transformation in both the history and the soul of mankind.

At the moment, we appear to be wedged between a traditional

secular system we are fast outgrowing and a spiritual system that we are currently busy shaping. The 'God Movement' is very much a people driven one. But there is "danger in the waters" as Jung once warned. We stand on the threshold surrounded by boundless new vistas of spiritual 'things'. Anything appears to go. The broad umbrella of today's New Age spirituality covers the globe, pagan religions as well as many of today's popular distortions of traditional religions. Someone could start off studying Buddhism meditation for example, then progress to yoga relaxation classes with a bit of 'hands on healing' and divination (ie: tarot card readings) tossed in for good measure– but ultimately end up with a mix of pantheism (all is god), monism (all is one), polytheism (many gods), paganism (trusting occult wisdom and powers), even neopaganism (idealized tribal cultures and pagan religions). An evil spirit tries to make his entrance as quietly and as unobtrusively as possible But be careful, the New Age movement is not the spirituality revolution. New Age surges far beyond... brandishing the promise of unconditional love, peace, power and personal transcendence and the movement presents a heady, alluring mix for the unsuspecting, the naïve and the vulnerable. It can lure many into unchartered and dangerous territories...When innocent people begin to dabble in witchcraft or psychic waters, they can open themselves up to a range of unsavory spiritual forces and anything can and frequently does, happen.

Unfortunately, in today's culture of 'scientific enlightenment', many people consider demonic possession and exorcism to be superstitious remnants of the Dark Ages. Even many Christians, contrary to the words of Jesus, scoff at the notion that the devil and demons really exist – despite Church dogma. Yet the Catholic Church still has senior official exorcists and every priest is ordained to perform exorcism, though mostly this ceremony is so special that it is left to the elite few within the Church whose services are quietly requested when the need arises.

The last recorded official exorcism in America took place at St. Louis in 1949 and involved a 13 year-old boy. The youngest priest involved in the case, Rev. Walter H. Halloran, who was called in to assist Frs. William Bowdern and Raymond Bishop during the ceremonies, died on March 1, 2005. The best-selling book and film 'The Exorcist' were loosely based on the real-life happenings and although the novel took some liberties with the actual events, Fr. Halloran had always maintained that during the releasement, among other signs of diabolic possession, he observed streaks and arrows and words like 'Hell' carved into the child's skin. To the end of his life, he was left in no doubt as to the 'real facts' of the situation: that they had been engaged in one almighty fight with the Devil himself.

With the vast majority of clinical psychologists currently keen to lay the blame for demonic possession at the door of mental instability, just what is the truth about exorcism? And why are we so fascinated by it?

From an energy perspective, the answer is quite simple. When fallen angels shape-shift they move from one mortal body to another, from one generation to the next. What is at stake is the human soul or energy body and demonic possession remains the fiercest of all battlegrounds in the war of light forces against dark.

Signs of diabolic possession include the speaking of unknown languages (often Aramaic or Latin, which are totally unfamiliar to the possessed person), the knowing of hidden or distant things and the manifestation of abnormal physical strength. Although each of these characteristics may, by themselves, be attributable to other causes and not necessarily signs of demonic possession, if they are accompanied by key spiritual 'symptoms', then the writing is very much on the wall, so to speak. These signs are: a vehement aversion for the name of God, the Holy name of Jesus in particular, the Blessed Virgin, the Saints, the Church, the Word of God, the sacraments, Holy Water, church incense and sacred images such as a Crucifix or holy pictures.

Some of the general rules concerning the rite of exorcism include obtaining the support and permission of the local diocesan bishop, finding a priest who is distinguishable by his piety, prudence and integrity and oftentimes locating a sacred place where the exorcism can be held in private. In addition to the ceremony itself, a crucifix should be at hand or somewhere in sight.

Many years ago, when I was a young 'adventurer' into the occult, I came across a woman, an inter-generational occultist on the left hand path, who could not bear to wear anything silver (silver being an especially pure and blessed metal used, alongside mercury, for the manufacture of bullets to kill vampires), who had a particular aversion to Churches and who would not enter a room if a Holy picture happened to hang from the wall. She simply could not and would not enter such premises, no matter what. If she had accidentally walked into an area where religious images were, she actually became physically very unwell. Just the sound of the name of Jesus was sufficient to cause her to depart. As a member of a clandestine satanic family that passed their occult practices down through the generations, this lady also happened to be a consummate liar and lies, as most energy workers know only too well, are the preferred strategy of the devil. He is a liar par excellence.

As Francois Mauriac wrote: "Evil is Someone, Someone who is multiple and whose name is legion…It is one thing to be in the realm of the demons…and quite another to be held and surrounded, literally possessed by him."

When our auras are depleted through tiredness, anger, fear or other negative emotions or activities, we lower our energetic vibrations, our protective auric shields shrink and we become susceptible to attack from lower astral entities.

Sadly, these dark energies do their utmost to hinder any kind of healing and can and do cause serious physical as well as mental problems – these painful illnesses providing them with 'fuel' to live on, until they move on to their next 'host'. Sometimes, sticky black etheric cords can be seen attached to the victim's aura, which is always affected being either torn, rippled or spiked. I have known of some individuals whose past incarnations have been so dark that they deliberately carry this negative energy over into subsequent lifetimes, opening themselves up to dark energy again and again.

It is no co-incidence that the majority of satanic families breed from one generation to the next and inter-marry with other families whose energy frequencies match their own. These groups take great care that their dark forms migrate untouched by the light of the Supreme Being through the karmic cycles of birth and death. They have no need to make physical contact with one another for they know each other on the Astral...

Of course, a denial of the existence of Satan and an acceptance of hitherto irreligious ceremonies (such as Halloween) as being both 'fun' and 'harmless' are just two ways in which human beings can make it much easier for demonic entities to gain a foothold. The British author C. S. Lewis in his famous 'Screwtape Letters' says something to this effect that if the little inexperienced novice devils, about to embark on their work of seducing men, can convince men that the devil does not exist, then half the battle is won!

On a recent trip to Australia in 2007, His Holiness the Dalai Lama spoke of this cosmic battle for men's souls. Evil, he warned the Melbourne audience of some 20,000 men, women and children, is making a great comeback. A refusal to deal with evil happenings is weakening the human race. "There are mischief-makers everywhere," warned His Holiness, "even in Heaven!"

Alcohol and drug use, as mentioned earlier, lower the auric shields we all have and leave us wide open. I know of some energy workers who will not touch alcohol expressly because of this. Sexual promiscuity is another avenue whereby demonic energies can enter. Sex industry workers are sadly typically prone to infestation by these forces as the act of intercourse provides the most basic platform for energy exchange.

Entry invasion is such a sensitive subject however that, when we are confronted with such horrors, we all too often, as Dr. Johnson once said, "take refuge in incredulity".

Satanic Ritual Abuse (SRA) of young children, for example, is a totally obnoxious and repellent subject. *Yet it happens.* What is our response? These unfortunate victims are scape-goated and labeled as mentally ill by a society that would rather not look at certain 'uncomfortable' things. But, as Dr. Timothy Taylor in 'The Buried Soul' has written: "SRA perpetrators and those who ritually murder children are, in a perverse and negative way, repossessing the power over life and death".

Children are totally innocent souls whose pure energy can be used to empower the possessed person. It is known that the ritual sacrifice of a male child born to a raped virgin occurs every Christmas Eve night, for example, among select covens around the world in a grotesque and hideous attempt to pervert the mission of the God-head. The child's mother is also murdered. These are unpleasant facts, but they are facts nonetheless. Ritual sacrifice can be the fate of many missing children lured unknowingly into satanic circles and the local police when stumbling onto the abandoned scene at a later date are always at a loss as to how to deal with such evil acts..

Although SRA is an extreme form of obsession and ownership by dark energy forces, demonic possession often happens in much subtler and less tragic forms than is supposed. Possession is much more common than most people ever imagine. And there are steps that you can take to avoid it.

Guarding yourself against unwanted invasion by negative energy forces is absolutely critical. By strengthening your auric field through a series of simple daily exercises, cutting etheric cords and pranic breathing meditations or prayers, you will protect yourself from these entities. Getting enough quality sleep, eating properly, listening to nature, meditating or praying daily, attending Church, laughing, having a more compassionate and loving attitude towards yourself and others, staying well away from negative people, and learning to defuse anger are all components of a healthy, vibrant and glowing spiritual body.

When you work to actively boost your personal energy space, you are healthier and happier, you will vibrate to a higher energy resonance and you will be part of a more dynamic world – above all, you will be a channel for Divine white energy, the energy that is God.

Alien Abductions or Demonic Encounters?

Far and away the most insidious form of energy manipulation of human beings involves abduction of the physical body by supposed 'aliens'. I use the word supposed because after all my years of research into this extraordinary subject I now remain convinced that these distressing cases of abductions, of so called 'walk ins' and 'wanderers' are the work of fallen angels.

As an energy worker, I have no doubt about either the validity or the sincerity of the individuals who have been violated by these beings from 'outer space'.

In interviews with renowned psychiatrists, many victims relate the same things – they describe their captors as having 'disturbing eyes', they report a feeling that such aliens think that they are totally superior to humans who, in their turn, report having absolutely no control over what was happening to them or what was about to happen to them during these encounters. A common sensation among victims has been described as one of total paralysis. One statement that cropped up time and again was the fact that most victims had come to the conclusion that the aliens are 'more advanced spiritually and emotionally' than humans. Almost every single victim was afterwards left with greater intuitive abilities in relation to other people than before.

One woman described how afterwards she could sense auric shields around others for example. Contact with highly evolved spiritual beings almost always results in some kind of energy transfer – such as the ability to read auras.

Only a very few had positive encounters and I have no doubt whatsoever that such was the case.

Yet to me all of these 'symptoms' are evidence of contact with highly evolved entities – *not aliens.* It would be very interesting to read the charka points of these victims. I have no doubt that these vital energy zones would be highly contaminated.

What I found profoundly disturbing however was the common thread that ran throughout the vast majority of these cases – and that is that abduction seems primarily concerned with the joining of two species for the creation of a new evolutionary form.

This is the Book of Enoch and the fall of the Watchers all over again.

According to the Old Testament prophet Daniel, these fallen ones are destined to rise up once more to mingle with mankind in the 4th and final kingdom (Armageddon) of the Beast (Satan). "They will mingle," writes the prophet, "with the seeds of men". (Daniel 2:43). The Bible goes on to further inform us that Satan and his followers reside in the first and second heavens (space) and that he (Satan) has 'dominion' (can actually exist) in this area. If viewed from the context of energy, this would make 'space ships' and UFOs highly plausible, as a shielding technique would be needed by beings on the left-hand path to enter earths highly charged spiritual atmosphere. What better avenue than science fiction!

When I spent time researching this subject, what became glaringly obvious is that *every single one of these abductions occurred on or within days of solar or lunar eclipses.* From an occultist standpoint, this is extremely significant, as eclipses remain the most magical of all times. They are symbols of cosmic power and catalysts for powerful rituals for *both energy transfer and regeneration.*

Places where UFOs are commonly sighted I have also found to be of interest. Map dowsing reveals that these areas are negative energy zones and hence are favorable 'spots' for dark force materialization. The Three Sisters peaks (ironically named Faith, Hope and Charity) in the Cascade Mountains of Central Oregon, USA, is such a spot. When we take into consideration that these peaks sit over a large area of negative underground water, we have an environment suited to negative energy materialisation

The mixing of genes started, as we have already read, with Cain's daughters, the women of Caanan who bore giants. In modern scientific parlance, when these females mated with the fallen angels they created a DNA defect called giantism. Bible Codes confirm small groups of fallen ones currently still in existence who are even now competing for dominance and control. Their aim is, quite simply, to breed the Anti Christ.

According to the Book of Jasher, past 'experiments' may well have resulted in the production of such beasts as the Pegasus, the Minotaur, even the dinosaurs. With this in mind, it is no surprise at all to find that the Nazis were totally obsessed with producing a 'master race'. *Their obsession makes total sense.* And if this is so, is this the more sinister side of modern day human cloning, I wonder?

But before you think that this is the stuff of science fiction or Hollywood as I did when I first started my research into this area, I would ask you to consider the case of Phil Schneider. Schneider, a civil engineer, was recruited to build a network of secret underground facilities for covert US government organizations to 'deal' with these aliens. He later disclosed that he left the 'service' because he became convinced that these 'aliens' were actively encouraging humans to move towards a one world government – run by themselves! Schneider was later assassinated in mysterious circumstances.

There has been much written on the subjects of 'walk-ins' and 'wanderers' – those among us who feel different from other people. In the case of 'walk-ins' we encounter individuals who bypass the normal karmic cycles of birth/death and whose energy bodies literally 'walk into' the physical form of a person who has just passed away. Such folk claim to have extraordinary healing powers and that their 'mission' is to bring compassion and peace to mankind. Sounds wonderful – however, I have a BIG problem with this. As an energy worker, I find it deeply disturbing that other energy beings simply 'hi-jack' the body of a dead human. *This is not the work of God.* Every single theological text – be it from the Koran, the Torah, the Bible or the Upanishads teaches respect for the dead and of the journeys that the spirits of the deceased must make. Inhabiting a human form without permission is not God's way. As for bringing to mankind messages of compassion and peace – what do we have the great religious teachings of the world for? I find such actions detestable.

As for 'wanderers' or so-called 'star people', I can only reiterate that such individuals are not white light workers or earth angels, I have come to the conclusion that these are none other than the 'offspring' of hybridization programs designed to people the earth with half-demonic half-human creatures. This has never been part of any Supreme plan. And never will be. Talk of bringing mankind to an intergalactic federation and of 'aliens' controlling all of earth's astral portals and gateways remains what it so palpably is – total and utter rubbish.

There is no doubt in my mind whatsoever that today the Veils of energy surrounding God are being attacked. The time has already come when many people have rejected the doctrine of God Almighty and have turned to false prophets and so-called 'Ascended Masters', even 'Beings of Light' who are nothing more than thinly disguised demonic forces – and all with one aim: deception. In fact, if Enoch is right (and I personally believe that he is), these 'star children' with special qualities, the products of hybridization, are already among us in their millions. They may be sitting next to you on the bus right now....

Halloween – not just a simple case of 'trick or treat'

Before I leave the subject of negative energy, I want to take a moment to discuss the subject of Halloween.

An ancient pagan ceremony held by Celtic druids to honour Samhain, lord of death, (pronounced so-wein), Halloween came to America via the large Irish and Scottish migrations of the mid 1800s. The festival itself runs roughly from sunset on October 31st to sunset on November 2nd and means quite literally 'summer's end'.

Samhain marked the beginning of winter and was the time when cattle were brought in from pasture to spend the winter under cover. The Celts believed that at Halloween the souls of the family dead were supposed to revisit their old homes to warm themselves by the fire and to partake of the cheer provided for them in the kitchen by their kin. (This has become the *Treat* so beloved of children today.) Burial mounds were opened and lighted torches hung on the walls to help the dead to see their way. To facilitate this and appease Samhain, druids rounded up cats, dogs, black sheep, oxen and human beings, stuffed them into wicker cages and burned them to death. On All Hallow's Eve, masks and disguises were worn; faces were blacked with soot and clothes worn inside out or back to front as a disguise and protection from evil spirits. (This became the *Trick* part of Halloween.) Later on, turnip heads containing a lighted candle (in America and Australia, the pumpkin is more readily found) were placed in windows to frighten off evil spirits. The lighted candle being a reminder of the Halloween bonfires.

Without a doubt, the most famous site for this festival remains Stonehenge in England.

As with all things light and dark, pagan festivals eventually became Holy festivals and it is on November 1st and 2nd that

Catholic countries celebrate the Days of the Dead and of the Holy Souls.

It is only in recent times however that Halloween has been reduced to a 'cultural' jollification for children but far from being a friendly fun-filled day, *it remains the day dark energy workers celebrate above all others.*

Satanists simply love Halloween. They receive a lot of favorable media coverage, which usually portrays them in a positive public light as seekers of 'spirituality'. The festival generates a lot of interest in dark magic and is good for recruitment purposes!

It is the night when those from the dark side meet in covens, drink, dance, spit out hexes and spells, conjure up and torture spirits, engage in orgies, induct new members and offer up animal and human sacrifices. I have always found it interesting to note that in the week before Halloween, many children go missing or are 'accidentally' killed. The remains of slaughtered animals in stone circles, or encased inside a circle, triangle or pyramid structure are often found afterwards by park rangers throughout America, Australia and Europe but such findings usually go unreported in the press. It is well known among light workers that Satanists have become expert at covering up their sacrifices – the use of incinerators on privately-owned land usually takes care of the bodies afterwards and there are, of course, deeply dug graves on such preserves as well as on private domestic-owned premises.

It is no coincidence that the Humane Society in the US refuses to release black cats during the time of Halloween for fear that they will be sacrificed. I think their decision is very wise.

White Light Workers & The Third Eye

Our journey into the dynamics of human energy fields would be incomplete without mention of the crucial role played by White Light Workers and the role of the Third 'All Seeing' Eye that, as multi-dimensional beings of energy we all possess, whether we have been tuned into using it, or not.

Einstein once said that reality is merely an illusion, albeit a very persistent one. And the 'reality' we all perceive every day through our five senses seems to be just that – real. But climb to the top of the nearest tall building and you will get a very different perspective of the neighborhood you inhabit. Looking out at the land far below you from the window of a plane, gives you an even bigger vista to absorb.

It is all a matter of perspective.

My feet are rooted firmly on the ground. My brain tells me this, because my eyes can see my feet. But when looked at from the spiritual or energy viewpoint, I might 'see' and therefore experience many more different 'things'.

Psychic abilities are a natural, fundamental part of who you, as an individual are. As children we all had our fair share of extraordinary dreams – the bed that floated up and away into the night sky, the magic carpet, the strange people and exotic places we encountered...But these are not just "dreams" or the results of an over-active imagination that our parents so casually dismissed. What is the magic carpet but astral travel? What are the encounters with others when dreaming but psychic conversations? Unfortunately, as we grow older we close off our sixth sense. But the world of spiritual energy is all around us *all of the time. Just because most of us cannot see this world, or feel it, or hear it, or smell or even taste it does not mean that it is NOT there.*

There are many very ordinary people whose faith in God, whose meditations, prayers, actions and daily lives are transforming the world in which we live.

These are the *White Light Workers* and they are very extraordinary people indeed.

Every spiritual tradition has 'birthed' them, so to speak and they remain impeccable beings who choose to take full responsibility for their state of existence. These Warriors Of Light have one mission only on this earth and that is to serve the Forces of Light, the Positive Spiritual Principles, with steadfast devotion to the Forces of Good. To achieve this, they have spent their incarnations mastering the means of spiritual protection from negative forces.

Western saints, eastern adepts, and indigenous shamans –these white light workers have united with the spirit of the God Head. They have ascended the cycles of karma and rebirth and have moved into that higher reality which is the eternal home of the soul. These mystical men and women have arisen in every age, from every culture and tradition and religion to inspire creative achievement in education, the arts, the sciences and even into the realms of government, believe it or not.

One of the most powerful white light workers I have been privileged to know is a humble tradesman whose knowledge and mastery of energy forces is phenomenal. When I come up against a particularly resistant and dangerous energy force, it is to him that I turn for help. It also happens that he is someone whom I have known in a past life and was guided to make contact with in this life under the most exceptional of circumstances. When we first met, I had the feeling that we had known each other before – which, of course, we had, though I had little knowledge of this at the time.

The spirit world works in a truly unusual way, its rules and regulations are fundamentally simple, its messages strictly of the telepathic kind and its frequency range is much higher than that to which humans are attuned. *To white light workers in the mortal realm, there is no such thing as 'coincidence'.* To this day, I do not know if an organized universal brotherhood of white energy workers exists, but I do know that when the time is right things move on the spiritual plane.

When I first received my 'awakening', it was the result of a series of gradual steps taken both subconsciously and consciously on the physical, astral, mental and spiritual planes.

Each time I 'changed gear', so to speak, my consciousness moved from one realm to the other and I experienced the sensation that 'happenings' on the physical plane are merely the result of those on the spiritual plane. For me, awakening was like a homecoming....

For children, the whirlpool of kundalini energy is absolutely natural, for the majority of adults tapping into this essence can be next to nigh impossible. We see if we want to see – or if our eyes (all 'three' incidentally) have been opened by a unique experience whatever that experience happens to be.

The White Light Guardians, or 'Occult Police' as Dion Fortune called them, function purely on the inner planes but there are White Lodges whose exclusive mandate is to combat Black Lodges. These White Lodges seem to have alliances in unexpected areas and to be able to pull together to exercise great power when necessary – for which we should all be very grateful. Some of these White Lodges were especially active in Britain and the US during WWII though very few people were aware of it.

Positive healing energy enters through the left side of the body and flows out through the right hand. When you tap into your psychic gifts, you not only activate your charkas, you raise the frequency of your energy body, your self-esteem and your fundamental trust in God – what you 'see', 'hear', 'feel', 'touch', 'smell' and even 'taste' is transformed.

As human beings we all have a gland called the Pineal. A relic of our former spiritual life, this tiny gland is located in the back area of the brain almost in the centre of the head and is referred to in energy circles as *the third 'all seeing' eye.*

Interestingly, the pineal actually looks like an eye for in some respects, it is literally an eyeball. It is round, connected together by ingrowths of white tissue and has an actual opening on it. In that opening is a lens for focusing light. This lens looks upwards, is hollow and has color receptors inside it. Just as our physical eyes can look up to 90 degrees away from the direction they are set, the pineal can also look as much as 90 degrees away from its set direction, which is always upwards. When activated, the color of the Third Eye is indigo merging to navy blue or soft purple. When I am in the presence of very dark energy my Third Eye feels this disturbance and I often experience a lot of headaches, blurred vision, and noises in my ears, even, occasionally, nightmares. Sometimes, an excess of energy can cause the pineal to temporarily close down. This is purely a resting period, when the gland needs to be recharged and realigned. With its reawakening, the adept is moved onto a higher psychic plane each time.

Hundreds of years ago, when homo sapiens was a much more spiritually evolved being than he is today, the pineal gland occupied pride of place in the human energy matrix. It was once the size of a table tennis ball. Today, with lack of use, it has shrunk to the size of a pea.

Yet, even in its pitiful shrunken state, this electrifying little eye, so beloved of ancient Hindu philosophy and yoga teaching, contains all the geometries and all the codes of creation. *In your mind's eye you possess all the secrets of the universe since time began. This incredible storehouse of knowledge is all there, in every single person.*

With The Fall from Divine grace, our spiritual memory banks closed down, we began to breathe differently taking in prana through our nose and mouth, instead of via the pineal and the crown chakra. As a result, prana bypassed the pineal and we 'saw' the world and our place in that world from a *totally different perspective.*

What became 'reality' became 'real', something tangible, and something that we could all 'see' with our physical eyes. The resulting 'blindness' to the reality of the spiritual world meant that we became energy beings trapped inside a physical shell looking out on a world whose complete and total 'reality' we were not fully participating in. With the dawn of the Age of

Reason and scientific 'enlightenment', we in the west almost closed the astral gateway permanently...almost...

When you activate prana through meditation, prayer, yoga or even special breathing techniques, for example, you start on a long-awaited journey back to the wellspring of who you as a multi-dimensional being of light energy really are. You stop trying to control your life, you actually let go and you 'let God'.

CONCLUSION

'Caro cardo salutis'
('It is in the flesh that salvation hinges')
Tertullian

As we come to the end of our overview of the human energy matrix, this may seem like rather an unusual quotation with which to sum up the first half of my work. But the words of Tertullian, an early North African theologian, are incredibly apt when attempting to describe the bridge between the twin worlds of body and the spirit.

In terms of energy, these are two disparate spheres, yet without learning in the physical realms (the world as we see it and know it), we cannot aspire to the spiritual. You could say that the physical is our karmic path to the cosmic energy (Tertullian calls this 'salvation') of the spiritual. The ultimate union of individual energy with the energy of the Divine is, of course, enlightenment and this is what the soul aspires to.

There is no doubt that we live in the midst of forces whose effects we can clearly perceive, but whose actions remain invisible to the vast majority of people.

For centuries, science has sought to explain the organizing principle behind the essence of life. Great minds have tried to unravel the secret of how life first began – but such men and women seek in vain for the answer will never be found on the physical plane.

Very occasionally though a spark of human genius will light up a small slice of the spiritual chasm and the world can catch a glimpse of the vastness of the spiritual energy that swathes the Universe. But the portal only opens a crack and the door soon closes...

Normally, we are protected from this spiritual world by our very incapacity to perceive these amazing energetic forces. Most of those individuals who choose to dabble in the occult are protected by their own lack of knowledge and scant experience. Yet today, we are almost saturated by mediums, psychics, and clairvoyants, even psychic detectives! All of these people are to some extent or another 'fringe-dwellers' on the spiritual planes. The spiritual domain is a perilous place for the uninitiated and the unprotected. But for those whose energies are destined to merge with the other side, the more contact there is with the spiritual realms, the greater the fusion of energy. Currents in the spiritual world run fast and deep. When I was awakened, for example, my past incarnations came back *en masse.* Some aspects were, quite frankly, terrifying, while other images were incredible and very humbling. When this happens, you never see the world in quite the same way ever again *and your life is changed forever...*

We can however meet the Unseen under some exceptional circumstances.

We can be in a place where these energy forces are focused and consequently run deep; we may have contact with certain individuals who handle such forces; we can, through personal interest, venture quite innocently into spiritual waters or we can become victims of energy that is used by others in a dark way.

Before the day began, the ancient Celts would draw an imaginary ring of protective white light around themselves to shield and guard them from the dangerous forces that lay ahead. My ancestors believed passionately that debts incurred in this life were carried over to the next and that wrongs committed and unpaid for would surely be avenged in a later existence. Many Celtic legends throughout Europe can only be fully understood in terms of acceptance of the reincarnation of the soul. Celtic myths specifically state that certain characters are reborn to live out a lesson from a past life. The ultimate purpose of these rebirths is, of course, knowledge and the attainment of wisdom. All bodies were said to belong to the earth and all returned to it at death. The flesh was not the *true* self even though it seemed inseparable. The spirit or *anamachara* was a teacher as well as a guide. The soul was the true self and this self gradually grew in wisdom through the cycle of incarnation.

In what must be one of the most exquisite of Celtic beliefs, it was said that when you really loved someone you shone the "light of your soul" on them. When two people came together, it was because their souls had recognized and acknowledged each other first...

To the Celt, the *soul* learned from and experienced the world, the seat of the soul was the heart, which harbored this knowledge; the *spirit* observed and guided the soul, and the *body* remained at all times the ship of the soul.

Wisdom and compassion remain the two truths that lead to the one truth and that truth is, of course, love.

Divine energy flows extravagantly to and from all living things. When the God-force first brought spirit to the earth, each individual was (and still is) destined to become an emissary of that spirit, raising the vibrations of the entire earth and merging with the energies of God.

As surprising as it may seem, even your own name carries a distinct energy frequency. Your name was not chosen for you at random by doting parents or, indeed, by chance! Certain indigenous cultures hold the power of names to be so precious that they will not give their real name to strangers – or even to the authorities. They know that your real name can be used against you – and this is true. Names are empowered with a unique vibrational quality that can actually steer you in a certain direction in life or indeed enable you to manifest specific characteristics. Your name is in fact your vibrational 'footprint', so to speak endowing you with special karmic knowledge and a range of other psychic gifts. Dark entities, for example, are destined to bear the same name throughout eternity – a name may be different but the spelling will be more or less the same. For example Katarina in a past life may be Katrina in this, and so on. Never underestimate the power of a name.

Today, humanity is returning home.

At this very moment in earth's history, the cosmic doorway is open – wide-open and the word of God is now evident almost everywhere on the planet. There are many different channels through which it comes.

The goal of human existence is – with all due respect to different religious beliefs – to purify the mind, to dissolve the 'ego' and to nourish within us the purest qualities of love, compassion, and respect for all sentient beings, spiritual strength and faith in God.

I believe with that we stand on the threshold of total enlightenment, total awakening – and that we are all participating in this process, whether we are aware of it or not. We are loved so extravagantly by a Higher Power, yet we do not know it. We are full of Divine loveliness and we refuse to believe it. We have the power to heal each other's wounds, but we remain in deliberate ignorance. Unconditional love is for so many people a veritable foreigner that most can never accept that this amazing gift can ever be bestowed on them. We have a strange resistance to the opportunity of intimacy with the Supreme Being....

"I have known both good and ill,
Sin and virtue.
Justice and injustice;
I have passed judgment

And I have been judged myself;
I have gone through
Death and birth,
Joy and sorrow,
Heaven and Hell;
And in the end, I recognized
That I am part of everything
And everything is part of me"
HAZRAT INAYAT KHAN

References:

1 The Concise Oxford English Dictionary, Oxford University press, UK, 2005.
2 'Thanks For the Memories'. ABC April 12, 2007.
3 Ravenscroft, Trevor. 'The Spear of Destiny', Weiser Books, Boston, USA 1982.
4 'Navy approves first ever Satanist', BBC Oct. 24, 2004.
5 'Angels Among Us', Time Magazine, 1993.
6 Freeman, Elias Eileen. 'Angelic healing: Working with Your Angels to heal Your Life'. New York, Warner Books, 1994.
7 'Airline Pilot Photographs an Angel', Weekly World News.
8 Milik, J.T. 'The Books of Enoch: Aramaic Fragments of Qumran Cave 4'. Clarendon press, Oxford, UK, 1976.
9 'Schools ban Potter 'occult' books', BBC Nov. 29, 2001.
10 'Vatican releases New Rite for Exorcism', Catholic World News, January 1999.

PART THREE:

CYCLES OF ENERGY – EARTH DRAGONS

THE EARTH IS BORN: THE DREAMING

'Where wast thou when I laid the foundations of the earth?
...when the morning stars sang together, and all the
sons of God shouted for joy?'
Job 38:4,7.

At the beginning of the world, there was only the "Dreaming"...

When the "Dreaming" ended, all things on the earth were formed – landscapes and great oceans, life above, below and in the world - and guardianship of the land was established. This is the *Altjeringa,* also called the Dreamtime. It is the essence of Aboriginal Australian tradition for it marked a time when ancestral creator spirits roamed the earth. Such spirits could change shapes at will and were said to have taken the forms of people, animals, plants even rocks. When they vanished into the ether, these beings left behind them 'footprints', visible marks on the landscape while the routes they took became known as 'Dreaming tracks' or 'song lines'.

It is always with a sense of wonderment and surprise when I come across a song line. Criss-crossing this great flat, dry continent, some lines are no more than a few kilometers long, while others extend for hundreds of kilometers and run through hills or plains, passing through the lands of many different Aboriginal groups each with their own unique cultures and codes of belief. The vibrations at these points are quite incredible. Magical. Breath-taking. Powerful. To this day, indigenous Australians believe that anyone born on or near a sacred Dreaming site is the incarnation of its associated being and is destined to become the guardian of that site. Ties to the earth for indigenous Australians run fast and deep and everything about mortal life is seen thereafter as an opportunity for spiritual awakening.

Other native traditions bear testament to the fact that every single site on the face of this earth has its own unique vibration, resonance and harmony.

The Middle East, for instance, is undeniably the spiritual and religious crucible of the world. It therefore comes as no surprise to find that this is an area of low magnetic density, which, in energy terms, means that these lands are subject to frequent changes and turbulence – as the history books show only too well.

In areas where higher magnetic readings occur, such as in Central Russia or China, change is not as rapid and the local population is usually slower to respond to new ideas, innovations etc. Though, when change does come, it tends to be far-reaching and transformative.

The great American psychic and healer Edgar Cayce (1877-1945) believed passionately that everything in the universe is vibration and went on to demonstrate that the collective energies of people in particular places or locations fused together to then create an energy or vibration all its own. The unique energies of this area in turn radiated outwards to attract others of the same vibrations to that area. Cayce once wrote: "Life in its manifestation is vibration." And it can be seen that regions of crime and violence attract the same dark personalities, whereas places where people pray, meditate or engage in powerful positive healing sessions are in their turn locations of deep peace and tranquility – even in the hub of a busy city.

It has been said that although energy can be transformed, it cannot be created or destroyed. This basic 19th century empirical observation has become known as the *conservation of energy concept.* But I would like to go even further and state that as a dowser, experience has taught me that there are some power points on the face of this earth that are better left completely untouched by mankind. These areas can resonate with either positive or negative force – *but their energy remains at all times so powerful that any kind of attempt to control, manipulate or transform them can have severe consequences.*

Such places can be either gateways for Divine energy, or portals for demonic energy. It is that simple. Knowledge of these 'gates' has come down to us through the ages. Certain pyramids of Egypt, for example, house this 'gateway' technology, as do specific holy temples and shrines. Secret messages encoded in ancient texts offer not only understandings of these astral doorways, but they provide us with important information as to how such energy operates.

We can learn much from the points of the humble compass. For instance, it is well known within occult circles that dark, malevolent energy enters from the north, whereas positive, pure energy runs along an east to west current.

As a dowser, whenever I come across a disturbing influence emanating from a power point, such as the site of an old temple, the immediate magnetic field must be taken into consideration. Most immediate fields possess a range of 12 to 30 feet, whereas the remote magnetic field can stretch from a hundred to three hundred yards. Power points of positive energy such as Glastonbury, Fatima or Lourdes have a much bigger magnetic field – stretching to a couple of miles and intersected with many leys of much force.

People living unknowingly close to or even on such beams of force will be always affected.

In January 1929, German scientist Baron Gustav von Pohl, a talented dowser who believed that earth radiations affected tree growth, animal behavior and human health, set out to prove officially that cancer deaths only happened to those people who had been sleeping in beds positioned above powerful water veins of negatively charged energy. In collaboration with the Berlin Centre for Cancer Research, von Pohl dowsed and recorded his findings in the town of Vilsbiburg, Southern Germany. Using his own Pohl scale of earth radiation, the Baron mapped the earth energy lines running through the town and then compared them with the death records held at the local district hospital. *Every single one of the 48 recent cancer deaths had occurred to people who had been sleeping in beds standing exactly above one of the powerful underground streams that von Pohl had mapped before seeing the medical records. There was no exception to this rule.*

In 1985, Dr. Veronika Carstens (wife of the former German Federal president Karl Carstens) published a study stating that there were 700 cases documented world-wide in which terminal cancer patients had regained their health without any conventional treatment after their beds had been moved from a geopathic stress zone. *All of these cancer patients had been given up by their doctors.*

While recently doing a spot of map dowsing along the waterlines of Melbourne, for instance, I discovered that *every single hospital* in the city has been built over negatively charged water veins. It did not matter how often I repeated the exercise, the result remained the same. When another colleague of mine was also asked (at my request) to perform the same exercise, the results were identical. Coincidence? I don't think so.

The question must be then asked – just what is energy?

For centuries mankind has attempted to discover and to define this mysterious substance that alone holds the key to who we, as a species, really are and where we actually came from. The philosopher Plato believed that our perception of the world was actually a shadow of the truth, while another Greek genius Pythagoras remained convinced that numbers were the language of nature. Even musical harmony and the movements of the heavens, as seen in early astrology, were said to describe this intricate interlocking of numbers and nature.

To this day, the theorem of Pythagoras remains the most important single theorem in the entire of sphere of mathematics. Developed around 550BC on the beautiful Greek island of Samos, Pythagoras held that the exact fit of numbers described the precise nature of the laws that bind the Universe. Later on, of course, as history tells us, this theory evolved into the Law of Motion, which, from an energy perspective is even more intriguing as to those involved in the dimensions of the spirit world energy moves in circles and waves...

But Plato too was near the truth for although we may 'think' that we perceive reality, what we in fact perceive is the *effects* of the vibrations that we encounter in our everyday lives.

Yet, despite the mathematics and the music – or maybe in spite of them, the spiritual dimension of the universe continually defies the neat building blocks of numbers and its very existence flies in the face of logic and reason.

Yet it was to be a physicist, Fritjof Capra, who in 1975 dazzled the scientific world with his book on energy: 'The Tao of Physics'. The main thrust of the work, which explored the link between quantum physics and eastern philosophy, was centered on the understanding of the universe as a dynamic interconnected whole.

Capra was fascinated by the fact that every single school of eastern mysticism believed that the universe has to be grasped dynamically as it moves, vibrates and indeed 'dances'. To the eastern holy man the cosmos quite literally teems with energy. Capra went on to write that the properties of sub atomic particles could *only* be understood in this 'dynamic' context – in terms of movement, interaction and transformation. For the average western student of science, this was not just a major break-through – it was a total revolution.

Later, Michel Gauquelin, the French psychologist and statistician, went even further. Gauquelin, who committed suicide on May 20, 1991, claimed that certain neural circuits in the brains of human embryos actually resonate in sympathy with specific planetary alignments and placements. In 'Cosmic Clocks' he put forward his theory, called 'The Mars Effect' and presented hard evidence to show that infants born while Mars is culminating or high in the heavens predisposed the child to athletics, where Saturn was prominent at birth, science tended to become of critical interest to the individual, a strong Jupiter placement equaled an attraction to the dramatic arts and political life, whereas most great writers and artists presented with a strong Moon placement. Picking up where Gauquelin left off, the English astronomer, Percy Seymour, went on to formulate a scientific theory for these astral influences to show that every human is affected by the "tidal tug" of the planets. Something in us, stated Seymour, responds to planetary alignments and movements – it is not the planet that makes the person: "rather the planets label a person's genetic predisposition to respond to specific magnetic signals".

There is no doubt whatsoever that we are exquisitely tuned to the magnetics of the earth. Every cell in the human body is a tiny electrical circuit transmitting, receiving and storing energy. Vibrations from the charkas become electrical signals that resonate throughout the physical body. It is now that the phrase: "You are energy" comes into its own.

The recently discovered specialized brain cell called the *magnetite* sheds a great deal of light on the matter. The cell is composed of chains of small crystals of magnetic iron oxide. These have been found in abundance in many mammals and birds – including humans - and enable us to tune into and *respond* to the planet's magnetic field. It is this cell that activates the universal Law of Attraction as popularized in the best seller *'The Secret'. Yet, the Law of Attraction is only one of many Universal Laws whose energy we remain largely unaware of. As incredible as it must appear, we use only a fraction of this amazing universal energy.* We now know that it is this energy that enables homing pigeons and robins to find their way when other cues such as the position of the Sun and the stars are not available. It is this structure that allows whales, dolphins, turtles, salmon and the like to navigate earth's seas, it explains why sheep sit in rows on ley-lines, invisible lines of energy that run all over the face of the earth and why cattle do not walk up-hill in straight lines. I also think that it is no mere coincidence that today mankind is experiencing an unprecedented spiritual shift in consciousness. The Spirituality Revolution is in the ascendance. But why? And why now in particular?

Scientific research reveals that the strength of the magnetic field that cloaks the earth is in decline. A reversal in earth's energy is happening right now. I do not believe that this is a mere geophysical phenomenon. As humans we are experiencing the vague sensation that things around us are changing in some fundamental way. They are...

With the gradual decline in earth's magnetic field strength though, each cell in the human body is slowly but surely responding to this great shift in cosmic consciousness. NASA's website features a map showing the gradual reversal of the north and south poles. What was once north will eventually become south, while the sun will rise and set in opposite directions. But whereas scientists look at the physical consequences of such a swing, energy workers look at the spiritual dynamics. If science is busy asking 'how?', healers want to know 'why?'.

The north magnetic pole currently resides in the Canadian Arctic – but at regular intervals throughout earth's 4.5 billion year history, both magnetic poles have flipped completely. A few thousand years prior to reversing, the planet's magnetic field actually weakens. Current records suggest that we are well and truly overdue for our next reversal, which tend to occur every 400,0000 years or so. The last time earth underwent a complete magnetic reversal it culminated in unusual extreme weather patterns as well as the destruction of Atlantis...With this current shift, the poles will, in effect, be returning to their original energy zones.

It is no coincidence that mankind is experiencing a spiritual awakening *at this very minute.* Every cell in the human body is vibrating to the coming of a new consciousness, a new spiritual baptism, a new relationship with the earth and ultimately with God who makes all things possible.

To energy workers, there really is no mystery - the world of the spiritual exists in perfect simplicity and harmony with the physical and its resonance is love.

'OM': THE FIRST SOUND IN THE UNIVERSE

"One must examine the sounds to understand the tones;
One must examine the tones to understand to understand the music.
He who understands the music can penetrate the customs and he who knows both customs and the music possesses the secret of life"
Da Dai Li Gi, Ancient Chinese Book of Customs.

If prana is the breath of life in the universe, then the sound 'OM' is the sole vibration of that free flowing force and the first step towards manifestation.

It has been written in many ancient religious texts that the world was in fact forged by this sound. In Christian, Hindu and Islamic scripts there are constant references to the music of the spheres – the heavenly music that gave birth to the universe, that maintains it and that will eventually dissolve it.

Sound is in fact so primordial I believe that it alone remains the creative principle. The breath of God became the voice of God – the "word" according to St. John that in the beginning formed the earth, the heavens and the stars. From the spiritual perspective, Genesis was a sound. A divine, procreative vibration.

'OM' (also written as 'AUM') is referred to time and again throughout religious scriptures as the supreme name for God. Different variations of 'OM' also lie at the heart of many different cultures and world religions – the Hebrew word 'shalom' (peace) and the Christian 'amen' ('so be it') being prime examples.

When the 'OM' mantra is sung during meditation, the tongue touches neither the top nor the bottom of the mouth. When chanted by Buddhist monks, for instance, 'OM' a continuous vibration that seems to come from silence, to be sustained by that silence and to return to silence.

'OM' is incredibly sacred and is said to represent the conscious world as well as the subtle realms and the causal planes (home of the ether). In its final stages, 'OM' becomes total and absolute reality. It neither arises, persists, nor perishes – it simply is...

The great Gothic cathedrals that are spread across northwest Europe were not just built to the greater glory of God, but are also structures for specific energy vibrations. If the human voice sounds different in an old church, this is because it *is* different. Hopi and Navajo shamans understood the deeper significance and origin of sound and would utter words into the sand to create intricate patterns. The complex yet delicate geometric depictions found in Hindu and Buddhist mandalas are used to alter states of consciousness – but they were first created in the sand by 'sound waves' made expressly by speaking the names of holy ones thus creating and holding the "vibration of God". In Tibetan Buddhism sand paintings continue to remain a strong feature of prayerful practice. Indeed a whole part of the ancient religious text, the Upanishads is devoted to the explanation of 'OM'.

But if spiritual disciplines have held the nature of sound special for thousands of years, science is a relatively new boy on the block.

According to this discipline, a vibration is defined as a motion of disturbance and because vibrations per se are not matter they can subsequently occupy the same space at the same time. Another phenomenon of vibration is *resonance,* which occurs when two objects emit identical vibrations. According to the textbooks, when energy is transferred from one of the objects via sound pressure waves, the other identical object vibrates in sympathy – because it has the same frequency. Thus the two objects *resonate as one.*

In 1967, Hans Jenny, a Swiss scientist, showed how sound vibrations created delicate and intricate geometric shapes. When quartz sand was spread thinly over the membrane of a drum and vibrated by various sounds, Jenny found that the most amazing shapes began to form. When low frequency sounds were played, they created a basic circle surrounded by rings, but when higher frequencies were played, the number of concentric rings around the central circle swelled dramatically resulting in a web of complex shapes such as tetrahedrons – mandalas and other sacred forms could also be seen.

Each frequency wave manifested exquisite geometric patterns in the sand. Changing the frequency changed the pattern. When several different frequencies were combined the patterns became ever more elaborate – rotational and spiraling movements resulted in shapes and forms identical to our own galaxies and solar systems. Some of the patterns found in crop circles, those mysterious patterns that appear in fields, were also clearly evident.

Although the 'Big Bang' theory may have started as a joke, this hypothesis may in fact be nearer to unraveling the mystery of creation than anyone in the scientific fraternity has got – thus far. In 2003 a US physicist, John Cramer, scrutinized data claimed by NASA to be heat radiation left over from the Big Bang some 13.7 billion years ago. When Cramer transformed the heat footprints back into sound, he came to the startling conclusion that the first sound was not so much a big bang as a giant *hum – a hum or an "OM"?* It does not take a gigantic stretch of the imagination to reach this conclusion.

As more physicists delve into the secrets of the universe, the results become ever more intriguing. Professor Adam Burrows of the University of Arizona has recently revealed that just before a star dies, it hums a note around middle C.

"It was so unexpected," Burrows later wrote, "that we kept rechecking and retesting our results. But we are now certain that this phenomenon...was sound waves".

When God brought spirit into and onto the earth, each living being on the earth was destined to become a 'messenger', a vehicle for that spirit. When the vibrations of spirit resonate, they raise the vibrations of the earth becoming channels of spiritual energy to all of mankind and we all move a little closer to the ultimate Source of all life.

CROP CIRCLES – SYMBOLS ON THE SKIN OF THE EARTH

"I am living to nourish you, cherish you.
I am pulsing the blood in your veins.
Feel the magic and power of surrender to life."
Uisce Beatha.

It comes as no surprise therefore to learn that crop circles, that extraordinary phenomenon of the last century, emit a frequency.

These increasingly complex patterns appear in the middle of fields of wheat – with no apparent trace of how they occurred. But as more and more of these circles (also known as 'glyphs') have appeared on the skin of the earth at specific locations, many researchers, mathematicians, scientists and circles 'watchers' have come to the conclusion that crop circles not only hum – they actually 'talk'. They are also orbits of strong healing energy – as many independent studies and personal testimonies have shown.

What I have found fascinating about these shapes is the fact that the greater the disturbance in the poles, the more crop circles that tend to appear. Also, these circles always form either on or near to those powerful beams of energy – leys.

Wiltshire in Southern England remains a major international

centre for these glyphs. Home to Stonehenge and the mysterious Avebury Stones, Wiltshire is criss-crossed by multiple arteries of ley lines. It is also 'home' to an incredible variety of ghosts, UFO sightings, numerous strange happenings as well as multiple crop circles!

To date, some ten thousand crop circles have now appeared in more than 20 countries in recent years including the US, Canada, Japan, Russia, China, Australia as well as the UK. Yet nothing about these beautiful sculptured shapes is consistent. They can appear with equal complexity in fields of barley, oats, wheat, and corn – even rice! From simple circular designs, they have grown in complexity to include precise geometrical designs. Without a doubt, the most intricate remains the *Mandelbrot Set* which formed in 1991 – a perfect representation of one of the most involved shapes in mathematics.

Despite some crude attempts by hoaxers, the glyphs continue to defy human replication. In fields of canola (rape seed oil), for instance, their manifestation is nothing short of miraculous. Canola has a consistency like celery. If the stalk is bent more than 45 degrees, it snaps apart. Yet, in a genuine crop circle, the stalks of canola are found bent flat at 90 degrees. They are not broken. There is no scientific explanation for this.

In a typical circle, plants are bent an inch above the soil, their cellular levels are altered and their stems are lightly burnt at the base. *Yet each stem is still alive.* The structure of the soil is fundamentally changed and the dowsable, electro-magnetic energies to the area are charged – so much so, in fact, that the effects on the human body are marked. In one case a British radiologist felt that he had been 'hit' by gamma radiation when he ventured into a local crop circle. He went home and fell into a deep sleep and the following day experienced tremendous mental clarity. Some cancer sufferers have had their tumors completely disappear, while medical evidence has shown that the Thyroid and Adrenal glands are beneficially affected after exposure to these formations. As both of these glands are the physical gateways to the Throat and base chakra points, the connection to a Higher Power feeding energy into Earth's grid simply cannot be ignored. Some photographers and researchers have experienced sudden, severe headaches on their Third Eye points. The pressure only eased once they had left the circle. Crop circles have the capacity to confuse compasses, block cellar phones and freeze batteries. And airline pilots crossing over the tops of these glyphs at an elevation of 500 feet commonly find that their equipment starts to fail!

Yet crop circles are not new.

As far back as 1678, we have several highly descriptive accounts of crop circle formations by a gentleman called Robert Plot, curator of Oxford's famous Ashmolean Library. And in the late 1800s there are eyewitness reports of crop circles appearing every few seconds. Currently, around 250 crop designs appear each year around the world.

But if crop circles are tangible evidence of a powerful energy moving across the face of the earth, of the earth talking to us, what exactly are they trying to tell us? Are they, as some believe, challenging the current worldview of 'reality' as we have come to know it? And, if they are, what is their significance for humanity?

In 1990, Colin Andrews, a crop circle researcher, showed pictures of some circle formations taken at Wiltshire to a group of North American Hopi Indians. When they saw a photograph of a glyph of the crescent moon, the elders were so shaken, they cried. According to Hopi tradition, it is said that humankind will know when the time of 'purification' has begun, through certain signs - one of which is the visible manifestation of the moon both on the earth and in the heavens. Later, that same year, on August 1, the second Gulf War, one of the most cynical conflicts of the last century, began...

Some mediums have talked about photon energy patterns hitting the earth's surface and thereby causing field crops to form patterns. Yet of the handful of eye witness accounts to date, all describe an 'invisible' force coming 'out of nowhere' in otherwise calm conditions and 'spinning' the crops down within a matter of seconds – usually with surprising force, yet little damage to the crop itself. Tornado-like funnels, balls of bright lights, sweet smells and high-pitched sounds have also been reported.

As public fascination with crop circles has grown, some national governments have attempted to publicly dismiss their appearance as a man made hoax. A few years ago, the British Parliament decided to do just this. On the morning following the Downing Street announcement, at the Prime Minister's official country residence, Chequers, a huge crop circle appeared. It had manifested overnight despite a significant security presence. No one, to this day, knows how it happened!

So, how are crop circles formed?

In my opinion, there is only one explanation for the formation of these incredible circles: sound.

High frequencies are known to affect human awareness and consciousness. The symbols inherent in crop circles emit specific frequencies. These high light tones, inaudible to most human ears, serve to channel light, healing powers into the complex energy grid that is the earth. If we look really carefully at the patterns and shapes on these glyphs, we will see that they are all connected, that they sit in perfect harmony alongside one another. This is no coincidence. When I dowse a crop circle, I feel continuous waves of energy surge through my hands and feet. I am also conscious of a high-pitched hum, a bit like a swarm of bees buzzing and there is always a tangible sense of the slowing down of time. After much meditation and research, I now believe that these shapes hold an intelligence to help move the human mind, body and spirit into another, higher realm of conscious awareness. They also have a message for us.

And that message is: We Are One.

To some, this may seem overly simplistic, even Utopian. Yet, there is little doubt that we are living in times of great spiritual transformation. If I had written a book like this one ten years ago, I should have been branded as a crank! Today, more and more people on the earth are coming to a realization of inter-connectedness. Together, we have a collective will. Whatever we do to one another, we do, in essence, to ourselves. This, of course, is not 'good' politics, but it is the essence of the human soul.

Crop circles lie on ancient energy paths. Along these networks our ancestors first built standing stones, then they built churches. For energy to move into the human consciousness, it must first impress itself into and through the energy grid of our planet. This, I believe, is the purpose of the crop circle. The crop circle is not logical nor is it rational. Above all, it is not scientific. It is quintessentially spiritual. *We must 'feel' our way through these energy fields.* Only then, will the 'mystery' of the crop circle be revealed.

SACRED SITES & STONES THAT TALK

"We are the Pilgrims...we shall go
Always a little further: it may be
Beyond that last blue mountain barred with snow,
Across that angry or that glimmering sea..."
'The Golden Journey to Samarkand, by James Elroy Flecker.

As humans, we interpret the world around us through our five physical senses of touch, taste, sight, smell and hearing. Indeed we have become so dependent on the feedback that we get from these 'senses' to filter and to limit to a manageable amount what would otherwise be an almost overwhelming input of data, that we have, in a way, become 'blinded' to the dynamics of the spiritual landscape, 'deaf' to its music, 'resistant' to its touch and its fragrance and utterly desensitized to its taste!

Yet, it must be remembered that these five senses operate on a wafer-thin band of frequencies existing in a universal and multi-dimensional spectrum of energy. The fields of vibrations that our primary and, some would say, primitive abilities fail to hear, see, touch, taste or smell is vast.

It is via our *intuition* – the sixth and, I believe, the most powerful of all of our human capabilities that we can enter fully into a dialogue with the spiritual domain. It is through this most fundamental of our senses that we can perceive and experience the interconnectedness of all things and that we can tap into an unlimited reservoir of information far above and below the range of our mere mortal powers.

Our energy body is miniscule compared with that of the world we inhabit. But each and every day we are in intimate and constant contact with the earth, exchanging not just water, air and food – but also, emotional and mental energy. *Today, despite the fact that we in the western world have largely forgotten how to achieve this balance, we actually continually engage in a spiritual relationship with the earth whether we are aware of it or not.*

And, while it is fashionable to talk in government circles about 'sustainability' and 'caring for the environment' in material, technological and economical terms, our ancestors successfully achieved a spiritual sustainability for thousands of years in their landscapes – even in the areas that they farmed. Their intuition guided them, prompted them, and told them that critical to their survival was this very special relationship between man and land.

They called this karmic essence: *Spirit of Place.*

The ancient Romans even had a name for this unique connection between the earth and mankind. They referred to it as: '*genus loci*' and often personalized this vital link, discussing it at length in their plays and poetry in colorful anthropomorphic terms.

Today in energy work, healers will often encompass the four vital earth energies: salt from the *earth* is used as a classic cleanser of negative energy, as are eggs; *water* from holy wells on sacred sites is used for purification, as is Holy Water from baptismal fonts; burning incense, aromatic oils, even herbs such as sage sticks, lavender and rue, sends smoke into the *air* releasing healing energies into the surrounding environment; while *fire* from candles or a bonfire remains a powerful transformer of energy.

If we could see this Spirit of Place through the eyes of our forbears, we would not only have respect for the earth, but the conclusions we would arrive at, our attitudes and subsequent behaviors towards the earth we inhabit would be completely different.

This unique spiritual relationship reaches fruition at various energy points or *Power centers,* as discussed in Part One. When we, as humans, place ourselves in these orbits of natural energy, we engage in the most profound and intimate way with the energies of the earth. These nodes on the skin of the earth replenish and strengthen human energy fields, healing and nourishing them and restoring damaged or dysfunctional parts to health and wellbeing.

But power centers are more than just exceptional places of healing energies.

These zones have their own cycles of time. They alone hold memory and information that has been fed into the earth's energy grid since the conception of the universe and their influence upon us is, consequently, much greater when we are present at these particular sites.

Through the act of *Pilgrimage* to specific holy places, we are in fact venerating these power centers. We 'read' their knowledge. We 'feel' their strength. Wherever we chose to go – to Lourdes, Fatima, to Mecca or to Tibet, we undergo a transformational journey of inspiration and healing at a deeply spiritual level. The pilgrimage itself marks a return to a spiritual focus enabling the pilgrim to engage in intimate dialogue with powerful and enlightening spirits.

All over the European landscape, there are *sacred wells* with the power to make barren women fertile and *holy wells* with healing properties, while other wells were used specifically for cursing enemies. At St. Aelian's Well at Llanelian yn Rhos in Wales, the victim's initials would be scratched on a tablet of slate, or written on parchment sealed with lead, and placed inside the well.

The symbolism of the *maze* or *labyrinth* is one of the oldest known to man and is believed to have originated in Egypt, from where it was brought to Europe by the Crusaders. At Chartres Cathedral in France, there is a stunning thirteenth century maze on the floor of the nave. Measuring 13 meters across, it has been built in such a way that if the wall housing the west rose window were to be hinged at the ground and bent down, the window would cover the maze exactly. Standing on the site of an ancient hilltop forest where local druids once performed religious rituals, the Cathedral crypt also contains a well once believed to have housed a representation of the Earth Mother.

Yet, mazes were more than just pretty pictures. To the ancient Celt, the maze served as a form of ritual for dance/meditation purposes. Mosaic labyrinths on the floors near doorways of Roman houses were symbols of protection to confound the entrance of evil spirits. While for the medieval citizen, mazes were representative of the fact that the path of the pilgrim was strewn with difficulties. Later on, during the seventeenth century, hedge mazes of increasing complexity were erected in the gardens of great villas – reflecting a popular concern with finding one's way to a goal. Mystics down through the ages have pondered the idea that the end of the spiral in mazes is also a beginning, a starting point. The labyrinth coiling back on itself was believed to house a two-way movement of spiritual energy – with angels or divine messages coming along one path, while the seeker after the truth (the pilgrim) headed off in another direction in pursuit of this knowledge.

The establishment of churches over ley lines means that these buildings in fact share alignments with heavenly bodies. In England during the 1950s, the Reverend Hugh Benson researched more than 300 churches and revealed that the vast majority aligned to the point of sunrise on the day of the saint to whom the church was dedicated, rather than aligning east, toward the rising sun and direction of the Resurrection! Twenty years later, Frenchman Lucien Richer mapped an extraordinary alignment of holy sites spanning Europe from the island of Skerrig Michael off the coast of southwest Ireland all the way to Mount Carmel in Israel. The route took in St. Michael's Mount in Cornwall, Mont St. Michel in France as well as Delphi, Athens and Delos in Greece. Along this very ley line are some of the world's oldest and most powerful sanctuaries to St. Michael the Archangel, standard-bearer for God in the fight against evil.

Even the basic layout of the Churches throughout the west houses an ancient, highly charged energetic symmetry. The Latin cross, the Cross of Christ, became the framework on which all Christian churches were built. Traditionally, a long nave led from the west toward a shorter chancel in the east, where the altar was located, while a transept formed the arms of the Cross.

The northern arm of the transept was associated with cold, darkness and evil and was usually decorated with scenes from the Old Testament, while the southern arm of the transept was identified with light and warmth and healing energies and was, typically, adorned with images from the New Testament.

The path of the nave represented a 'passage' or a journeying along a sacred space to the altar. Taken from the Latin: 'Navis' for 'ship', symbolically, the nave carried the worshipper to the altar – the symbol of Christ's life – where he or she was then 'altered' by being in the presence of Divine energy.

In the eastern Mediterranean, the Byzantine church focused the attention of the visitor on the majestic dome – which was identified with the vault of heaven, floating in the sky above.

When I dowse these holy sites either in person with L-rods, or remotely with my pendant, I am amazed time and time again at the sheer power emanating from them. After hundreds of years, the feet of pilgrims and worshippers has worn hollows and dips into the solid stone steps and paths that run through these buildings, showing that every single one of these places of worship remains a catalyst for powerful personal transformation.

When the pilgrim puts the soles of his or her shoes to the soul of the world, it means getting back in touch with our earth, our spiritual roots, and, ultimately ourselves.

Today, more people are setting out on pilgrimages than at any time since the Middle Ages. From the ancient pilgrim roads of Santiago de Compostela (known simply as 'The Camino'), to Jerusalem, Mecca or Rome, millions of seekers are returning to sacred sites to find something that in the hurly burly of the modern world, they seem to have lost. They are returning to spiritual sources to be restored and rejuvenated.

The *Camino*, for example, is more than just a destination to venerate the bones of the apostle, St, James. This particular pilgrimage is essentially a grueling 800-kilometre trek from France across the Pyrenees to Santiago in the northwest corner of Spain. St. Francis of Assisi, the Holy Roman Emperor Charlemagne, Dante even Geoffrey Chaucer have all trekked the *Camino* which follows an intricate and highly charged web of leys that, quite literally, enable the pilgrim to commune with the Higher Reality we know as God.

Some journeys, such as those to Mecca for the *hajj* can take even longer and may use up a lifetime's savings. As Mecca is the point of intersection between the vertical axis reaching up to Heaven and the horizontal plane of human existence, for the pilgrim, the journey is priceless.

In the Path of the Dragon: Stonehenge

Standing resplendent on Salisbury Plain in England against the rich, verdant backdrop of the rolling Wiltshire downland is Stonehenge, the giant circle of megaliths. It is only when you approach Stonehenge itself with the stones silhouetted starkly against the sky, that the true size of the place becomes apparent and even the most casual of visitors can not help but be struck by the awe and wonder of the site. But if Stonehenge by day evokes a sense of inspiration, by night (and especially during the time of a Full Moon or the winter solstice) it becomes a totally different place...

As an engineering feat, Stonehenge compares with the Great Pyramids. The giant uprights, or *Sarsens,* are more than thirteen feet high and weigh at least fifty tons each. It is now known that some thirty of these, surmounted by massive lintels, were originally arranged in a thousand-foot circle. Inside this, there was another circle consisting of some sixty 'bluestones', each weighing about five tons; and inside these, a horseshoe, also of bluestones. Finally, in amongst these, lay another horseshoe of five vast 'trilithons'.

Though debate still rages as to how the stones were put up and where they originated from, for me the most important question about this mysterious sight remains: *why were the stones erected in the first place?*

It is surely no coincidence that across the European landscape at about this time – in France, Sweden, Spain, Portugal, Malta, the Hebrides and in Ireland – there appear to have been a rash of similar monuments being built. France alone has about 6,000 standing stones, including the immense avenues of stones at Carnac, Brittany – a thousand of them set up in lines totaling some four miles in length. Cornwall on England's west coast is quite literally full of these monuments – including Boscawen Un, which is said to be the oldest stone monument in Britain.

There has always been the vague assumption that these

massive stone edifices were pagan religious sites, but apart from this hypothesis, the real reason for their construction remains an enigma. Were they vast calculating machines, whose chief purpose was to predict the eclipses of the moon and the paths of the stars? Or were they, as author Erich Von Daniken has suggested, somehow tied up with 'visitors from outer space'?

In 1968, film director Stanley Kubrick's *'2001: A Space Odyssey'* gripped the public's imagination and popularized the notion that extra terrestrials played a key role in the development of the human race. When Von Daniken's book: *'Chariots of the Gods'* made its international debut shortly after, the world was stunned by his assertions that the pyramids were built by spacemen (on the grounds that they were too massive to have been possibly built by human hands), and that the various markings on the face of the earth, such as the Nazca Lines, were giant runways for alien spacecraft! I find it incredible that Von Daniken can have reached these conclusions not the least of which (in the latter instance) is because the most powerful modern aircraft does not actually need a runway several miles long! Besides, if UFO reports are anything to go by, alien spacecraft land vertically – as our own spaceships do.

I am not an archaeologist nor am I an obsessive UFO follower. I am a dowser. And as such, I track energy frequencies both within the matrix of sentient beings and within the earth. When I look at these ancient giant monuments, the one thing that constantly intrigues me is *the sheer power of the stones*. The force is so great that my dowsing rods, even my pendulum respond immediately.

There are legends of dancing associated with these megaliths and Stonehenge itself was originally called the 'Giants' Dance'. Why? And why are tales of dancing linked so persistently with all of these stone circles? There are even myths that the giant megaliths on the Wiltshire downs are in fact men and women who were changed to stone as a punishment for dancing on the

Sabbath! As with all legends, however, the truth is never far from the actual myth. After many years of research, I have come to believe passionately that all of these stone monuments, built as they are on powerful arteries of earth energies (leys) are nothing less than giant 'conductors' that could be charged (a bit like batteries) to store as well as to release potent earth energies. The act of dancing, in this instance, would serve to 'stimulate' such electrical forces, drawing them up from the earth. And, although there is no mention of singing in historical documents, it is probable that besides dancing, participants may also have chanted as well, thus boosting the natural electricity already present at the site.

In traditional Chinese medicine, needles are placed at specific acupuncture points on the body. The aim is to stimulate and direct the flow of chi, or vital energy within the patient thus correcting imbalances and restoring overall harmony and health.

In more or less the same way, these ancient stones act as 'needles' stimulating and directing 'chi'. *I now believe that this, and this alone, is the sole purpose of these giant structures.*

In South Dakota, US, there is a megalith known as Standing Rock. It was common practice for Sioux Indian medicine men to press their spines against it to revitalize their powers of telepathy, healing and clairvoyance. In many indigenous cultures there are special sacred stones, even wells or groves, where human beings could merge with earth energies to tap into and to activate psychic forces. In Brittany, local women continue to embrace the standing stones to ensure fertility, while children still crawl nine times through the Men-an-tol stone in Cornwall to cure rickets. Medieval poets speak of Stonehenge as a healing oasis that drew all sorts of people to restore their health.

I think the poets were right.

Ground Zero

But, if such power can be potent, it can also be dangerous, as mentioned in the earlier part of this chapter. Negative water veins running underneath homes can cause illness and dowsers can be drained and exhausted by such immense forces. When I am in an area of such energy, I always feel a building up of tension, followed by dizziness and often, disorientation. The Roman historian Plutarch (45 – 125 AD circa) cautioned: "Men are affected by streams of varying potency issuing from the Earth. Some of these drive people crazy, or cause death, the effect of others is good, soothing and beneficial".

Indeed, whenever a place has had prayers and concentrated positive thoughts directed at it, it forms, as Dion Fortune once wrote "an electrical vortex that gathers to itself a force" – a force that can be used to benefit mankind.

However, when an otherwise positive energy field has become stressed and traumatized – such as at Ground Zero in New York, for example – the flow of healing vibrations is disturbed, blocked and sometimes even knocked off course. The doors to the spirit world are also closed. Such imbalances can be corrected and through dowsing, the areas concerned can be restored to harmony once more. As humans, we can always enter into a spiritual dialogue with such places and, as conductors of positive earth forces, dowsers can work to reconfigure the basic nature of earth's subtle body in a gentle and respectful way.

If positive healing were to be applied to Ground Zero, for instance, many trapped spirits would be released to the Light and New Yorkers would soon find that this area of their city would once again become a place of lightness and a great symbol of peace in their nation.

ASTRAL GATEWAYS & PORTALS TO THE WORLD OF MEN

"And how, pray, did you come to enter my dominion?"
"Please, your Majesty, I came in through a wardrobe."

"A wardrobe? What do you mean?"
"I – I opened a door and found myself here, your Majesty," said Edmund.
"Ha!" said the Queen, speaking more to herself than to him. "A door. A door from the world of men. I have heard of such things."
The Lion, The Witch & The Wardrobe by C.S. Lewis

In C.S. Lewis' classic children's saga 'The Chronicles of Narnia', the major protagonists Peter, Susan, Edmund and Lucy enter into the realm of another, magical world, Narnia, through a door in a wardrobe and begin a series of adventures that will change their young lives forever....

Since time immemorial, man has been fascinated by 'gateways' to other dimensions – nearly the entire discipline of science fiction writing is consumed with this concept and it has provided much scope for Hollywood movie directors over the years. There are numerous doorways linking Middle Earth to the planetary surface throughout Tolkien's 'Lord of The Ring' Trilogy. And who can forget the elusive Shangri-La, so beautifully described by the novelist James Hilton, and accessed only via a special 'door' in an otherwise impenetrable mountain range?

But do astral doorways really exist?

The answer is a resounding: 'yes'.

I speak from personal experience when I say that there are major portals, vortexes and dimensional doorways at specific points along earth's energy grid that serve to connect this world to other planets and stars in the universe. Some of these gateways carry positive, healing energy from a Higher Power. Others, most definitely do not.

A few years ago on the eve of a Red or 'Blood Moon' eclipse at about 1.30 in the morning, our family dog decided that she needed to go to the toilet urgently. I let her out into the back garden and went off to make a cup of tea. About half an hour had passed and there was still no sign of the dog. So I went to the door and called her. As the moon was waxing full, the light that particular night was very bright and I could see the dog clearly just sitting in a corner of the garden staring fixedly at some point in the distance. As it was very late, and not wishing to make any further noise by calling out to her, I walked up to her and simply brought her inside. She came quietly and willingly. But, as we were walking up the porch steps to go back inside the house, the dog froze and stared intently once again in the same direction. This time, I looked up too, as I wanted to know what was bothering her so much. To my complete astonishment, I saw a huge black 'doorway' (there really is no other word for it) in the driveway of the house next door. It was rectangular in shape, totally dense (the deepest black I have ever seen) and it completely obscured everything that it covered. I have never seen anything like it.

I quickly put the dog inside and then walked round to the front of the house where I could have a better view. The 'gateway' or 'door' was still there as big and as dense as ever. The shadows cast by the near full moon were in the opposite direction, so there could be no misinterpreting this phenomenon as a shadow. What was so unusual about this object was that, unlike the trees and shrubs around it, *it cast no shadow.*

The following morning during my prayers and meditation, I was given the message that this was a 'door'. Later on,. I checked with a healer colleague. He told me that this was a portal, that Australia is quite literally teeming with them and that these particular ones are not static or fixed in any way. He also said that the portal would be gone by the Eclipse. He was right. The following night, there was no trace of it at all.

Like chakra or acupuncture points, portals are vortexes of spiraling energy. The force they contain moves clockwise with gravity, and anti-clockwise with anti-gravity. Dowsing reveals the existence of powerful crystals within the earth that serve to receive, transmit and assimilate energy sending it out along the matrix or grid that maps the surface of the world. Leys bear the concentration of this force and it is along these pathways that special nodes (as marked by holy sites and crop circles) and openings (where portals, gates or doors) flourish.

The sole function of these interdimensional passages is to link our world to the universe and, ultimately, to the source of all life, God.

But there are also gateways that lead to darker, subterranean undercurrents.

Many old Indian burial grounds seem to act like portals and, for reasons that remain unknown to us today, indigenous Americans consciously located their burial grounds in places that they felt aligned to the after-death realm. Evil spirits who had taken human form (or humans who had become possessed by them) were buried face down at specific locations of negative energy, so that they could not return to trouble the living. The Amityville house of horror was built over one such site. No amount of cleansing can ever heal these areas. These sites should remain undisturbed.

Whereas the portal I saw was by no means 'fixed', and was without a doubt a doorway into the dark dimensions, other gates most definitely are fixed.

The Bermuda Triangle is such a portal.

But it is by no means the only one. In 1972, researcher and author Ivan T. Sanderson set out to examine and record many of these zones that exist around the world. His research brought to light a series of other similar Bermuda Triangle tragedies (in the same vein as the Marie Celeste 'ghost ship', for example) scattered across the globe. Indeed some of these sites were even located hundreds of miles from any water! In the final analysis, Sanderson found that the Great Lakes area on the border of the US and Canada has an even higher concentration of unexplained ship disappearances than anywhere else in the world, while Hanging Rock at Victoria's Mt. Macedon in Australia remains a doorway to a parallel universe.

Controlled studies done around suspected portals have revealed that there are definite temperature fluctuations in the vicinity of the site, while photographs taken often produce amazing results. Individuals sensitive to psychic fields report a feeling of 'magnetism', as if they are being drawn into the gateway, while some even see large numbers of entities moving back and forth. For those few individuals who have ventured inside a portal and have returned, life on earth seems to have little meaning. Some have even gone completely mad.

Perhaps the nearest that science has come to understanding the dimensions and sheer power of these gateways involves the mystique of *Black Holes.*

Technically speaking, a black hole is an area of space which appears absolutely black because the gravitation in the hole is so intense that not even light can escape into the surrounding areas. Such a dense mass produces a gravitational field that is strong enough to pull everything within its vicinity into it, while at the same time, allowing nothing, not even light, to escape from it. What happens to an object that passes through the 'event horizon' of the hole is even more fantastic than the wildest science fiction. If the black hole is not rotating, the object will be pulled directly into the centre of the black hole to a point, called in physics, the 'singularity'. Once there, it will literally be squeezed out of existence – or, as the physicists say, to zero volume!

At the black hole, singularity of all the laws of physics breaks down completely and even space and time disappear. It has been speculated that everything, which is sucked into a black hole, is spilled out again on 'the other side' – the 'other side' being another universe!

Many psychics believe that housed within some of the earth's ancient pyramids and holy sites, there remains special 'gateway technology' enabling travel between heavenly and earthly realms. In Genesis, we see Jacob dreaming of a ladder set on the earth and reaching up to the gates of Heaven, with angels ascending and descending on it. In 'Gateway to the Gods', author Craig Hines invites readers to reconsider preconceived notions of Biblical theology in the light of recent scientific discoveries and inquiries concerning the nature of the universe. Drawing together a variety of historical sources and backed by years of meticulous research, Hines has put together a compelling and strong argument about the validity of astral portals.

As humans, we remain fundamentally unable to move back and forth across the doorsills of these portals. The reason is that our physical bodies hinder us. In meditation or astral travel, however, we possess the capability (as did Jacob in the Old Testament) to pass through these realms, returning safely back home when dawn breaks.

HOLY RELICS – HEAVEN ON EARTH

'When in April the sweet showers fall...
Then people long to go on pilgrimages
And palmers long to seek the stranger strands
Of far-off saints, hallowed in sundry lands,
And specially, from every shire's end
In England down to Canterbury they wend
To seek the holy blissful martyr, quick
To give his help to them when they were sick.'
The Canterbury Tales by Geoffrey Chaucer, circa 1386.

Thus far, we have seen that both people and places emit special energy frequencies, so it should come as no surprise to discover that certain 'objects' possess this magnetism as well. To anyone trained in the esoteric arts, it has long been known that certain relics possess special power and, further, that such power can be harnessed and used for whatever means the current owner chooses.

At this stage, I would like to point out that it is the *intention* behind the force that makes that force itself either 'white' or 'black'. While to hold such power, gives the 'magician' influence over those who do not, it is critical to understand that this power works *at all times* solely within the laws of the universe. In other words, what is given out will return eventually to the sender.

The most obvious example of the use of holy relics for evil purposes remains that of the Third Reich.

As far as most historians are concerned, the rise to power of Adolf Hitler and the Nazi party in Germany during the 1930s was both an historical and a political fact. Some academics have alluded to the Third Reich's origins in an occult sect, to the occult beliefs of certain top Nazi officials, to the mystical rites of the SS and the Hitler Youth Brigade – *yet none has ever given serious consideration to the vital role the occult played in German politics during the Second World War. In fact, British Prime Minister at the time, Winston Churchill was so insistent that the occultism of the Nazi Party and its search for holy relics should not under any circumstances be revealed, that one is left asking the inevitable: why? And why did he give permission for a secret squadron of elite soldiers, under the command of Captain Walter Thompson to track down some of these special relics in Nuremberg – just months before the final collapse of the Reich?* (1)

The truth is that the Nazi Party, headed by Hitler, was an entirely occultist movement. And the evidence for this is everywhere.

'One Reich, One People, One Fuehrer' is a standard reflection of the threefold power circles of the occult, whilst self-denial, brotherhood mission, fearlessness of death and psychic knowledge were all widely employed within the Reich. On one floor of Wewelsberg Castle, the SS training school, for instance, is a dark mosaic star over which select Nazi officers known as 'The Twelve Knights' performed magical rituals. The Castle has recently been opened to tourists who can see these obvious signs and symbols for themselves. Hitler even ordered that quasi-magical Sig runes were to be part of any typewriter keyboard made in Germany, while the Ahnenerbe, a special division of the SS, were commissioned to roam the world to find proof that only one race was meant to rule the earth and that the Nazi vision of purification and world domination was indeed supported by mythical forces.

Heinrich Himmler, Hitler's Reichsfuhrer SS, saw the men in his army as the reincarnation of the Teutonic Knights of old, whilst the ultimate goal of all inner members of the clandestine black magic order, the Thule society (to which Hitler belonged) was to merge the divine self with the unseen realm of the spirit, to tap into the universal energy field to 'awaken the sleeping powers within'.

Even the Nazi salute: "Sieg, Heil!" meaning, "Glory, Hail!" is first and foremost a response to salute a god-man! Yet nowhere are these occultist tendencies more pronounced than in the fanatical search by Hitler for holy relics such as the Ark of the Covenant and the Holy Grail.

Whilst to millions of people around the world, relics have the ability to save souls and to heal bodies, for this elitist group of Third Reich initiates, only specific relics held the power to facilitate the establishment of a New World Order. And they were relics that the Nazis simply had to have....

Relics have long been known to provide victory and protection.

The bones of St. Cuthbert, for example, were carried into battle by the armies of William the Conqueror during his bid for the English throne at the battle of Hastings in 1066; and the arm of St. Fillan, present at the famous battle of Bannockburn, is credited with helping Scotland secure her independence from England.

In the Middle Ages, a church law stipulated that all altars had to have at least two relics, while a cathedral of any status was reputed to possess one part of the True Cross.

Yet, the Roman Catholic Church did not invent the veneration of relics.

In both Buddhism and Confucianism, the worship of body parts, even the hairs of masters, is an ancient practice that remains active in contemporary times. In 2002, a tooth of the Buddha was given a warm welcome during a special seventy-six day visit to Thailand!

There are numerous witnesses to testify to the fact that some statues of the Virgin weep, that hosts used during Mass bleed and that the wearing of a scapula (a tiny portion of a saint's clothing) can heal. That sacred relics have 'lives' of their own goes without saying and many of them pass through the hands of different 'owners' before finally reaching their current abode. In the very hour that the Spear of Destiny, for example, passed from a German vault into the 'ownership' of a liberating American army, the spear's former holder, Hitler, committed suicide. The new official owners of the spear, the US, then went on to unleash the horrors of the world's first weapon of mass destruction: the atomic bomb and the nuclear age was born...

Here is a snapshot of some of the most enigmatic relics in the history of the world and just why they are so powerful.

The Ark of the Covenant

In Exodus 25:10, God tells Moses to make a box of acacia wood, two and a half cubits long, one and a half cubits wide and one and a half cubits high. It was to be decorated inside and out with pure gold, while two pairs of gold rings on either side were to support poles of acacia wood to be used to carry the ark. On top of this chest, two cherubim, formed out of one solid piece of gold, sat facing each other, wings fanned out at either end of the lid or 'mercy seat'. Inside of the ark, we are told that Moses placed the stone tablets of the Ten Commandments that God had given him, the Torah he had written, the almond wood staff of Aaron, the high priest, that had mysteriously budded and a golden pot of the last trace of the heavenly manna that had sustained the Israelites during their 40 years of wanderings in the desert. "There I shall come to meet you," God says to Moses and adds:"I shall give you all of my commands for the people of Israel".

These words come from one of the most significant events in the entire history of the Jewish people and also present us with the greatest object of devotion in all of Israel – the Ark of the Covenant. The Ark is so much more than a simple box made out of incorruptible wood. It represents the beginnings of a people's national identity – from slavery to freedom and asserts their position as the people who chose God. The Lord's presence with the Ark was a constant reminder that God would not abandon His people to suffer slavery ever again. The Ark of the Covenant is the Ark of the Lord of all the earth. It is God in a box.

The Old Testament is replete with horrible stories of the terrifying power of the Ark. Those who accidentally violated it by touching it were instantly struck down, while the Philistines, who managed to hold onto the Ark for seven months after inflicting a crushing defeat on the Israelites, finally brought the Ark to Cariathiaim where the Jewish people were allowed to recover it. In the wrong hands, it seems, the Ark caused immense death and destruction.

Depending on who is searching for it, the Ark has now been lost for some two thousand years, and has been, alongside the Holy Grail, possibly the most sought after sacred relic the world has ever known. Almost everyone from Knights Templars to Hitler and even Indiana Jones in 'Raiders of the Lost Ark' has searched in vain for this incredible vehicle of power. The reason is obvious: the Ark has an intimate connection with the Divine. It is the one and only object through which God revealed His presence as well as His great power. To the Jewish people the Ark stood at the centre of the whole world on the standing point of the creation. The Ark is the stuff legends are made of.

But what exactly is the secret power of the Ark?

Once again, depending on whom you read, the Ark is either a 'super weapon' or a 'radio transmitter for talking to God'.

The Old Testament paints a vivid picture of the Ark playing a pivotal role in assisting the Jewish people in their conquest of Canaan by parting the Jordan River, as well as causing the walls of Jericho to tumble. The Ark's 'supernatural' powers to repel undesirable foreign forces, as a mighty weapon of warfare, are legendary.

Von Daniken has written that the Ark was an alien invention that was electrically charged and claimed that if the Ark were to be reconstructed today, according to the original instructions as handed down to Moses, that a voltage of several hundred volts should be produced. Exact models of the Ark have been produced, albeit on a much-reduced scale, according to the very specific Biblical specifications, *yet none has produced even a single spark!*

This is because the real energy of the Ark lies in its association with God, in its link with the Supreme Being. The Ark is definitely not a radio transmitter!

A note in the standard issue of the current Israeli Bible states that: "The Law of the Lord will be written in the heart, and there will be no need to keep it in the Ark". The Ark points to a truth that is timeless – that the all-powerful energy of God exists for now and for always. It is not confined to a box.

The search for the Ark continues however and rumors abound as to its whereabouts. To some it is located in a secret chamber buried underneath Temple Mount in Jerusalem, to others it is safely stored in France, or Ireland, or even in Scotland. While Ethiopians remain convinced that the Ark is in their possession and each year nearly 70 million locals celebrate this 'ownership' during the *Timkat,* a passionate celebration combining the feast of the Epiphany and that of St. Michael, the nation's favourite saint.

When I dowse over these areas, I find that the strongest readings for the energies of this extraordinary relic emanate from Temple Mount in Jerusalem. There is no doubt that the rock underneath the Temple Mount is a very sacred place. The rock itself is a huge natural table into which the original Phoenician builders made large cuts some 2,500 years ago. But it is what lies underneath the rock that so intrigues me. There is a veritable honeycomb of underground passages and natural caverns. Today, a stairway still descends from the temple to the cavern and excavations during the 1980s revealed a network of secret passageways and tunnels. *Remote dowsing reveals that the Ark is in this area.*

Today, the Temple Mount is in Islamic hands and the authorities will not give permission for the Mount to be explored.

The Holy Grail

Like the Ark, the quest for the Holy Grail, the cup used by Christ at the Last Supper, has been going on for at least a thousand years.

The subject of much western literature, poetry, prose and plays, the Grail remains one of the most hunted relics of all time.

Known also as *The Sangreal,* legend has it that this cup appeared to King Arthur and the Knights of the Round Table in Camelot amid a strange dazzling light in which they saw each other more wisely and more generously than ever before. The Grail itself was shrouded in white samite and in the form of a Chalice of the Mass. According to the myth, the vision rendered them all speechless.

To seekers of the Grail, the very quest itself is synonymous with the development of the inner soul from a form of somnambulism to spiritual awakening. Interestingly, the word 'grail' stems from the word 'graduate', which means gradual, or step-by-step thus mirroring the process of inner spiritual transformation that this Cup engenders. The Grail has also been described as a precious stone (Lapis Excellis), which is linked to the Third 'all seeing' eye. Once this Eye has been activated, the hidden secrets of time and of human destiny are revealed.

To ancient Celts, the Grail was represented by the Cauldron of Bron – a source of endless bounty; to medieval alchemists, the Grail became the Philosopher's Stone – the stone that fell from heaven with the power to turn base metals into gold.

In 1938, top German archaeologist and respected Grail historian, Otto Rahn, was busy searching for the Chalice in the south of France – claiming that it was a "source of indescribable magnitude". Soon after the publication of his book "Crusade Against the Grail" in 1933, he caught the attention of Himmler and was induced to assist the Nazis in their explorations into ancient civilizations and treasures.

To the occultists, the Grail is a symbol for hidden knowledge. For Hitler, the "real virtues" of the Cup of Christ were: "common to all the best Aryan peoples. Christianity only added the seeds of decadence such as forgiveness, self-abnegation, weakness, false humility and the very denial of the evolutionary laws of survival of the fittest, the most courageous and the talented". (2)

Australian journalist, Stephen H. Roberts, described the colored pictures he saw displayed in Munich for short time during the autumn of 1936: "of Hitler in the actual silver garments of the Knight of the Grail". Roberts afterwards wrote that he believed that the reason for their sudden withdrawal from circulation was because "they gave the show away…(and) were too near the truth of Hitler's mentality".

Whilst the Nazis spent a great deal of time trying to recover the Grail, there are those who believe that the Cup is unobtainable, while others believe that the Grail was never actually lost and is in fact in safe keeping somewhere in France or Spain, or even in England. Some historians and researchers go so far as to state that the Grail is not an object at all – but is the bloodline of the family of Jesus, the *Sangre real*, or Sacred Blood, despite a wealth of evidence that proves otherwise.

The Spear of Destiny

With the exception of the burial shroud of Christ, the Spear, which pierced His side, commands a great deal of public attention – especially as, just like the shroud, it can still be seen today. Also known as the Spear of Destiny, it is held in a museum in Vienna, Austria.

In the closing chapters of Saint John's Passion narrative, we are told of how a soldier pierced the side of Our Lord with a Spear. The centurion's name has been recorded as Gaius Cassius Longinus and he attended the Crucifixion of Jesus as the official representative of the regional Pro-Consul, Pontius Pilate. We also know that Gaius Cassius had cataracts in both eyes and that this had prevented him from being on active service with his Legion. Instead, the veteran officer had been assigned to report on the religious and political scene in Jerusalem.

For nearly two years, the centurion had followed closely the activities of Jesus of Nazareth and later, at the foot of the Cross, he watched horrified while a party of Jewish temple Guards started clubbing the limbs of the two other prisoners beside Christ. The Evangelist tells us quite clearly that to prevent this happening to Jesus, the centurion rushed up to the foot of the Cross of Christ and pierced His side (between the fourth and fifth ribs) with a spear – a mixture of blood and water poured forth and, in a moment of miraculous healing, the sight of Gaius Cassius was restored.

Back at the temple, where senior members of the Sanhedrin waited for news of the mutilation of Christ's body, the Veil of the Holy of Holies was split in two exposing the Black Cube of the Ark of the Covenant – the birth of Christianity, the new Covenant, had begun...

Legend has it that the centurion later made a gift of the

solitary iron spearhead to Our Lady and that he became one of the first gentile converts to Christianity, seeking instruction from Christ's disciples at Caesarea. Afterwards, it is said that Gaius Cassius spent his remaining years in Cappadocia converting pagans to Christianity before his martyrdom at the hands of the area governor.

Many myths have grown up around the Spear and it is said that whoever possesses it and who understands the powers that it serves, can hold the destiny of the world in his hands – for good or evil. The choice is in the hands of the holder, literally.

Of all of the relics in existence today, only one embodies totally the idea that man himself is a bridge between two worlds – the earthly and the spiritual, and that relic is *the Spear.*

It can be viewed at the Treasure House of the Hofburg Museum in Vienna, in the self-same spot where Adolf Hitler first beheld it as a penniless and starving artist in 1909.

Today its ownership has passed into the hands of the USA. And its influence has been tragically all too obvious. In the Cold War era that followed the collapse of the Nazi empire, the US has been involved, at great personal cost to her people, in several doomed conflicts such as Vietnam and Iraq. As the years have gone by, its leaders appear to have moved away from the noble ideals of former post war President Dwight Eisenhower to a country whose interests are now under the total domination of multinational corporations that stalk the globe with their own personal agendas – human cloning, genetic modification of the food chain and absolute domination of fuel supplies.

In the right hands the Spear is an incredible force for goodness and Light. But when used to empower the owner for personal gain, the full horrors of the dark side of the Spear are unleashed.

The Shroud of Turin

Without a doubt the most famous relic of them all remains the burial shroud of Jesus – otherwise known as the Shroud of Turin.

For believers, the Shroud is not just a burial cloth, it is evidence of the Resurrection of Christ, the Son of God. And, on the rare occasions when it is on public display, the lines of people eager to catch a glimpse of it can stretch for many miles.

Since 1578, the Shroud has been kept in the Italian city of Turin, in the Cathedral of St. John the Baptist. Its journey to the city however has been a long one and, in common with most Holy relics, the burial cloth has traveled from the Near East to Constantinople in Turkey, to France and finally to Turin – where it remains.

The property of the Pope, the Shroud is remarkably well preserved and measures some 4.36 meters in length and 1.1 meters wide. It weighs approximately 2.45 kgs. In 2000, to mark the Great Jubilee of Redemption, John Paul II, who called the Shroud "the mirror of the Gospels", allowed a special screening of the Shroud during the Easter season.

Despite all of the debate about its authenticity, the Shroud still remains an enigma.

While armies of scientists including chemists, pathologists, physicists – even biblical scholars and art historians remain in disagreement over it, no-one can explain just how and why the perfect image of a crucified man remains…Recent analyses have shown that grains and pollens identified as exclusive to the Jerusalem region and to be found only in the months of March and April places the cloth's origin in or near Jerusalem well before the 8th century.

On the cloth itself the marks of wounds on the left wrist, right foot and right side are clearly visible. There are signs of severe flogging over the whole body – administered by a three-corded instrument with pieces of lead attached to the ends of the ropes. Such flagellation would have produced multiple contusions and severe lacerations. Jewish practice limited scourging to 39 lashes – but Roman scourging was unlimited and the only rule amongst the soldiers doing the whipping was not to kill the victim. Roman lashers thus became experts at keeping their prisoners alive...

The forehead and top of the head of the man on the shroud are marked by rivulets of blood provoked by sharp pointed thorns. As this was not the usual method of Roman torture, the only documenting of the use of a crown of thorns remains that of Our Lord's Crucifixion. *It was a totally unique event in crucifixion history.*

There are large chaffing marks on both sides of the upper back area in the scapular region consistent with the carrying of a heavy crossbeam (the patibulum) across the shoulders. A typical patibulum could weigh anything from 50 – 100 pounds (45.5 kgs). If there was more than one victim to be executed, a standard Roman practice was to tie a rope connecting the ankles of the victims and the ends of the crossbeams – preventing the victims from running away or swinging the beam to hit a soldier.

Although the Scriptures do not specifically state that Jesus fell three times, Christian tradition has always strongly supported this. Evidence from the Shroud reveals dirt on the knee, the left eyebrow and left cheek, damage to His right eyebrow and the center of the forehead and on the tip of the nose – all consistent with a series of heavy falls.

The nail wounds on the Shroud appear to be through the wrists and the feet and are indicative of seven-inch iron nails commonly used by the Romans. Recent pathologist reports show that there are two divergent streams of blood on the forearm which relate to two angles of blood flow from the changing position of the arms on the cross as the victim lifted himself up to breathe and then dropped back down again. On the shroud, the left foot is lifted up over the right foot and a large single nail was driven through it.

Further evidence has shown that *the legs of the man on the shroud were not broken, while there is evidence of a lance wound to the ribs.*

The crucified man has been estimated to be about 35 years of age and 180 cms tall.

But far and away the most mysterious and inexplicable part of the shroud is the fact that the image of a crucified man has remained clearly visible down through the centuries. Scientists have pored over the cloth and have come to the conclusion that the image is literally *burned onto the shroud from some power or energy emanating from inside the cloth.*

As the Son of God, Jesus has been described as 'the Light of the World'. At the Transfiguration and again, at the Resurrection, the Gospels tell us that Christ's face "shone like the sun", that his clothing became brilliant like "lightening" (Luke 9:29). Jesus possessed a Divine power that, as mortals, we simply cannot understand, let alone quantify in clinical scientific terms. Surely only incredible light energy could have imprinted such an image?

The face of the figure on the Shroud is haunting in its serenity – even in death and such an agonizing death at that, it remains majestic.

Today the Shroud lies in a climate controlled conservation case at the Cathedral at Turin. Showings depend on the Pope and are rare events.

CONCLUSION

"I consider compassion to be the basis and supreme support of humankind."
His Holiness the Dalai Lama.

Buddhists believe that subtle particles existed in space long before the creation of the universe. *And that these particles are still there.* Worlds, say followers of the Eight-Fold Path, may come and go *but* the 'spirit' that composes the universe remains. Space, however we quantify it, is definitely not empty.

Throughout the course of this chapter, we have examined the earth as a multi-dimensional field of energy, whose vibrations, like the great blue oceans, are constantly moving and ever changing. We have learnt that we, as sentient beings, are an intimate part of all that we can experience. And, in a way, we are just so lucky. For every day we have a unique opportunity to live in harmony with the energies of the earth and ultimately of the universe – as opposed to ruling and attempting (rather foolishly) to control creation. For no matter how hard we try to do this, creation always ends up ruling us! Who, for instance, can catch a wave or bottle cloud? It is impossible.

There is no doubt that we are highly evolved and powerful spiritual beings and, in many ways, we are the creators of our own experiences. But, as we can see, the energy matrix of the universe shows that we are but 'sparks' of a divine, creative intelligence that is responsible for our very existence.

I believe that this extraordinary creative energy is God.

It has been said by some authors that we can rebuild a 'new heaven and a new earth', but I would say that we must learn to embrace the quality of compassion. For without this nothing is possible. The 'new heaven' and 'new earth' as prophesized by the Evangelist John in Revelation come into being when the energy of God dwells "once again within man". And this energy makes all things new.

The great standing stones that our ancestors built on the skin of the earth, the massive cathedrals and other sacred monuments and the amazing appearance of crop circles – all of these things, when studied in their proper light with an understanding of their reason for being – show us that when we are in tune both with God and with the energy frequencies of the planet, we represent one great fusion of energy.

The single most important lesson from this world of spirit is to have compassion for every living thing. When we fill our lives with this quality, the way we think changes, our relationships with one another blossom, even our ability to sustain love, surely the hardest of all human emotions, changes irrevocably. Tears are wiped away and pain is no more.

The key to compassion involves walking in the light. Once a light shines in the darkness it can never be switched off. Ever.

As we have seen though – especially in the section on relics – dark energies are constantly tailing light ones. This 'electricity', if you like, seems to be part and parcel of the nature of life in the universe. In the apparitions of the Virgin Mary, Our Lady has told visionaries that whenever she and Jesus appear, so too does Satan. When I am dowsing an ancient site I will always feel the tug of both of these forces, but I am fully aware of the fact that no matter how dark the energy at a particular spot may be, that the light vibration is, and always will be, stronger. This is the nature of positive Divine energy.

All of the pain that you may experience in your life, all of the love, anger, frustration, joy, rage, jealousy, laughter, even disappointment – the entire spectrum of human emotions allows you, as a being of light energy, to help you to know yourself. When people have stood in the middle of a freshly formed crop circle, they have experienced a multitude of disparate feelings, by releasing the negative sentiments and embracing the positive ones, they can and, very often do, turn their lives around.

This is when healing takes place. When we mediate in silent contemplation – or sometimes even express great anger to the Supreme Being for an action we simply cannot fathom, we are, in essence, tuning into an incredible and inexhaustible source of energy. And, if we let it, this source can transform our lives. No one can live permanently in a state of anger, for instance. If the anger is repressed over many years, the person will manifest a chronic illness and will leave behind them an imprint of that anger on their immediate environment. One of the first emotions that I feel when I am dowsing a negative site is anger. But, if we choose to let that anger go, to release it and to have compassion on the individual who may have been the cause of that anger, we let the waters of forgiveness flow and we find peace.

This is when miracles happen.

When we corrupt the earth with indiscriminate use of toxic substances, choke the skies with greenhouse gas emissions and create the appalling slaughterhouse conditions of intensive farming methods, this is when the spirit of the earth cries out against man.

This is when natural disasters happen.

The earth is ever forgiving and ever compassionate. Our ancestors lived in harmony with the natural cycles and rhythm of nature. Nature respected man and gave richly of her bounty. Today we burn fossil fuels and cut down trees. We call this progress. The earth calls it a holocaust.

When will we learn?

As the dawn breaks every morning, and as the sun sets each night this earth shows us that we are indeed eternal beings. The energy that transcends creation also flows through us. We do not need a new heaven, or a new earth – they exist already.

This is the lesson of the compassionate earth.

References:

1 & 2 Ravenscroft, Trevor. 'The Spear of destiny', Weiser Books, Boston, USA. 1982.

EPILOGUE

AS IT IS IN HEAVEN

"The People that walketh in darkness have seen a great light".
Isaiah.

In 1944 during a heart attack, the great Swiss psychologist Carl Gustav Jung had a near death experience.

He later wrote: *"Far below I saw the earth bathed in a gloriously blue light. I saw the deep blue sea and the continents. I could see the snow-covered Himalayas. I knew that I was at the point of departing from the Earth. The sight of the earth from this height was the most glorious thing I had ever seen".*

Life is indeed beautiful and like Jung, I too feel the exquisite glory of the earth.

As I look out now onto my large and rambling garden awash with early morning dew and fog still clinging to the tops of the tall majestic gum trees, a Rainbow Lorikeet calls out to other parrots nestled in the surrounding trees and then is still. For one magical moment, there is total silence...I am reminded of the hauntingly beautiful world we inhabit and I am so grateful to God for all the wonderful things He has given me – even the pain, the sorrow and all of the hardships. For, it is through the prism of these experiences that I have come to know and to believe in the reality of a Higher Power. The power of the Trinity. It has been said that a gift of love from the Creator can sometimes be wrapped in pain and throughout all of my experiences hitherto with energy, I see this 'movement out' from personal tragedy and grief towards light and love time and time again in the lives of those with whom I have come into contact..

This is spirit in motion.

The 12th century Benedictine visionary and mystic Hildegard von Bingen (1098-1179) called this action *Viriditas*. Roughly translated from the Latin it means 'greening of the soul' by the sacred life force of God's spirit. According to Hildegard, God's breathing of *viriditas* into Adam and Eve conferred on them both the gift of life – not of death. With their fall from grace, *viriditas* did not diminish but continued to flow from one human being to another as a river of spiritual life.

When you see reality through the eyes of spirit, you will rise (quite effortlessly) above the physical world and you will come to realize that this material existence is not only devoid of meaning, it is a hollow creation filled with fear and confusion – and, it has to be admitted, only transitory contentment at best.

The world of spirit, on the other hand, is the world of light and true life. It occupies a realm whose currency is one of total peace, a peace Jesus says that the "world does not know".

Only spirit is permanent and only spirit endures.

When my teacher George had a NDE, he was shown several different spiritual environments. He saw the earthy dimension in which all living things (humans and animals alike) were bathed in electrically charged multicolored force fields (auras). Alongside the physical world, he witnessed the existence of a *grey, colorless dimension* where souls without auras couldn't or wouldn't leave the earthly plane. Some of these beings were bonded to others though love, but others were clearly earth-bound by compulsions, drug, sex or alcohol addictions and they gravitated towards living beings with similar patterns of behavior. When humans drinking in a pub or at a bar got drunk, George could see gaps opening up in the electrical fields surrounding their bodies, then he saw these grey souls rush in suddenly to experience the sensation of getting drunk.

The next area George was shown consisted mostly of those colorless souls who appeared to be lost, yet also to be totally consumed by their own innate selfishness and attachments to material things. My friend later described these beings as amongst the most 'hateful know-alls', 'bitter' and 'angry' souls he had ever encountered.

Throughout all of these dimensions, George said he both felt and saw the presence of angels trying to offer help and sometimes even getting through to these souls. George was keen to let me know that these angels "don't have wings". Yet, he was also profoundly aware of another 'presence' – an energy form that he later described to me as a bright and compassionate light – a light that could feel all things. George said that the light seemed to know everything about him and that this incredible being loved him in spite of the wrongs that he had committed during his life. He was also acutely aware that the achievements that he considered to be important milestones during his time on earth actually mattered very little to this being of light energy. "Things such as hugging a crying child, extending a helping hand to those in need and expressing love counted for so much more," he told me afterwards. When these things were shown, George saw that the light being radiated the most intense white light he had ever seen. George's mind flashed back to the teachings of Jesus and he recalled the phrase: *"I am the light of the world. Whoever follows me will never walk in darkness, but will have the light of life"*. He wondered if this New Testament script was reflecting what he could clearly feel and see?

It was then that George knew that he was in the presence of Jesus Christ.

Rather than sounding strange to us, the idea of God, the Creator, being light makes more sense than ever before.

In the opening to his Gospel, St. John writes: "In Him was life and that life was the light of men". He uses the Greek word *zoe* which, roughly translated, means 'divine life' or 'divine spark'.

What John is writing about is the nucleus of all energy on earth and in Heaven. This Spiritual energy is the spark of life itself. The ancient Hebrew word for 'spirit' is *ruwach* meaning 'breath' – the breath of life that God in Genesis breathed into all things...

But, be warned, dark entities and forms simply cannot sustain an impression of bright white light. One of the ultimate deceptions played upon mortals by demonic forces is this very mask of the "lightness". For adventurers into the world of healers and exorcists, discernment of spirit is crucial. It is no coincidence that Satan is frequently referred to by the Virgin Mary during her apparitions at Medjurgorje as 'the shining darkness'.

I once knew a 'healer' who claimed proudly to her unsuspecting and immensely wealthy clients that both Jesus and Mary appeared to her every day! It later transpired that her 'apparitions' were from the dark side, as indeed was the healer herself.

If, in times of crisis, you can rise up and walk in the path of God, trusting in His Supreme Power, the adept from the Left Hand Path will have no power over you whatsoever – regardless of the fact that you may have no knowledge of the occult.

This is one of the many mysteries of the universe.

Isaac Luria remains one of the most influential Kabbalists in the history of Jewish mysticism. Luria, known as Ari (the lion), lived in the sixteenth century. His mystical insights were so captivating that he changed the course of Judaism dramatically and permanently. One of Luria's key teachings centered on the belief that every particle in the universe is a shell that contains sparks of holiness. Our function, he said, was to release each spark from its shell, raising it up to bring it into harmony with the universe. The way we accomplish this 'raising' is through acts of loving kindness...

We all have this potential to raise holy sparks and everything you will ever do in your life will present you with this unique opportunity.

If humanity could do "on Earth as it is in Heaven", I have no doubt that we could all connect to a power beyond ourselves and far beyond the confines of the human imagination. As beings of

Free Will, we can separate from God, going our own way in our karmas, or we can choose to be guided by the Light of the Creator.

This quintessentially human struggle is either won or lost on a personal basis every single day.

We can listen to the *small, still voice of a Higher Power, or we can choose to walk into the grayness of life that eventually becomes swallowed up in the darkness.*

The choice is ours.

Now tell me, what path will you choose to walk today?

"May the road rise to meet you.
May the wind always be at your back.
May the sun shine warm upon your face,
The rain fall soft upon your fields,
And until we meet again,
May God hold you in the palm of His hand."
AN IRISH BLESSING

GLOSSARY

Akashic Records The universal database of the past, present and future of every soul on earth. It is here that the soul is shown the model plan of its life to be lived, the people it will encounter and the places it will journey to. The Records state that it is the destiny of every soul to realize the presence of God in a set time and place in the world.

Alignment The movement of energy to attune with personal desires.

Altjeringa The Australian Aboriginal word for 'Dreamtime', a time thousands of years ago when Aboriginals believed that their ancestors roamed across Australia creating the landscape and all living things.

Anamachara The ancient Celtic word for 'spirit', the energy force that guides the human soul.

Angel In Christianity, Judaism and Islam, a messenger of God.

Astral Travel The ability of the spiritual body to traverse the universe at night while the physical body sleeps. Often called 'out of body experience'.

Auras Auras are fields of magnetic energy that surround every living thing. For humans, auras comprise of six various sheaths of which the etheric body or shell is the easiest to see.

Bardo Thodol The Tibetan Book of the Dead, a manual for guiding the soul of a deceased person safely through the dying process.

Black Hole An area of space that appears to be completely black because the gravitation in the hole is so strong that it pulls everything within its vicinity into it – including light.

Black Magic Also known as 'The Left Hand' path or the 'Dark Arts', Black Magic seeks to dominate and control others for the purposes of empowerment. The black magician derives his or her particular power from the Devil.

Blood Moon When the moon passes through the earth's shadow gradually turning a dark copper color. On a spiritual level, this phase marks an ending and changing of energies and signals a time of chaos.

Black Lodges Organizations dedicated to the dark arts.

Bible The Christian holy book, divided into two parts – the Old Testament (Jewish writings) and the New Testament (the story of Jesus and his teachings).

Buddha A great teacher who lived in northeast India sometime between the 6th and 4th centuries BCE. Followers use his teachings as a guide through life.

Buddhism An ancient faith based on the teachings of the Buddha. The Four Noble Truths (on the nature of suffering) comprise the foundation of Buddhism and it is said that they cannot be absorbed or learned – except by personal experience or insight over several lifetimes.

Chakras These are whirling vortices of energy at the conjunction point between mind and body. Sited in a rod-like formation over the spine, they resemble 'spinning wheels' as spiritual energy (prana) courses through them. They are the most intimate interface between the physical and spiritual realms.

Chi Also known as "Qi", Chi is the Chinese word used to describe the concept of energy or life force that flows throughout the Universe. When Chi gathers the physical body is formed, when it disperses, the body dies.

Chika The moment of death.

Chonyid The experience of reality.

Crop Circle Mysterious complex patterns that appear in the middle of fields of vegetation such as wheat, oats, barley or corn. The stalks are squashed down flat over a large area, with no trace of how it happened. Also known as 'glyphs'.

Dalai Lama The title of the leader of Tibet's Buddhists. The words mean 'ocean of wisdom'. Due to the political turmoil in Tibet, the present Dalai Lama lives in exile in India.

Demon An evil spirit or devil.

Dreaming, the – An Aboriginal belief about a time long ago when the world was made.

Enlightenment An understanding of the true meaning of life.

Feng Shui The ancient Chinese practice of living in harmony with the environment.

God Also called 'The Supreme Being', the 'Creator' or 'The Divine', in many religious beliefs God is a great, all-knowing, all-seeing force who created and rules the world, mankind and the heavens.

Halo A glow of divine energy visible around the head.

Halloween An ancient pagan ceremony held by Celtic druids to honour Samhain, lord of the dead. In recent times, Halloween has become a major 'cultural event' in the West. It is the day dark energy workers celebrate above all.

Intuition The sixth human sense enabling dialogue with the spirit realm. An innate and often inexplicable feeling of right or wrong. Immediate insight.

Kabbalah Jewish mysticism.

Karma The universal law of cause and effect.

Ki In Japanese 'breath of life', Ki is the energy that moves through all of creation. Similar to 'Chi'.

Kundalini Sacred energy that resides curled up at the base of the spine. When kundalini is awakened, enlightenment is said to occur.

Labyrinth Also known as a maze, the labyrinth houses a two-way movement of spiritual energy – with angels coming along one path, while pilgrims walk another path in search of greater knowledge of God.

Ley Lines Invisible spirit lines that criss-cross the earth. Sometimes visible in places as 'tracks'.

Magic The art of influencing the course of events by occult control of spirits and other forces.

Magnetic Density A way of measuring earth's energy fields.

Areas of 'low magnetic density' are subject to frequent changes, whereas areas of 'high magnetic density' are slower to respond to change.

Mudras The positioning of hands during prayerful meditation.

Magnetic Cell Chains of small crystals of magnetic iron oxide found in many animal species known to possess a magnetic sense.

Meridians In China, meridians are energy channels throughout the body along which prana runs. Known as 'Nadis' in India.

Monism A belief that all is one.

Near Death Experience Where a spirit has crossed over to the astral realm and then returned back into the body.

Negative Thought Form Commonly used in psychic attack, a negative thought form is the result of negative thinking (anger, jealousy, revenge etc.). It is deliberately sent to inflict harm.

New Age A diversified movement begun in the 1980s aimed at promoting a new worldwide view based on a blend of human ethics, holistic health ideals and traditional eastern religions. The New Age philosophy is that there is neither ultimate truth nor a personal God.

Nirvana In Buddhism everything that rises can also cease. The complete cessation of 'Dukka", the state of suffering, is Nirvana.

Occult The study of magic.

OM Sometimes written as 'AUM', OM is reputed to have been the first sound in the universe. It is commonly believed to be the word of God that formed the world and every thing in it.

Paganism The veneration of the Mother Goddess and the natural world.

Pantheism The doctrine that God is everything and everything is God.

Polytheism The worship of many gods.

Portals Vortices of whirling energy at set points on the earth that act as gateways to the astral planes.

Power Centers Points on the earth's skin where powerful positive and negative forces converge. The result is an energetic fusion with an immense capacity to inspire, transform and heal. These centers are often 'spiritual doorways' for the adept.

Prana Divine energy that flows through every living thing and that returns to God when mortal life has been extinguished.

Pretans In Tibetan Buddhism, Pretans are incarnations of hunger, thirst, craving and frustration.

Psychic Attack The conscious manipulation of energy forces to deliberately harm or kill.

Reiki The ancient Japanese art of 'hands on' healing.

Resonance Occurs when two objects emit identical vibrations.

Ritual An activity that follows a set procedure aimed at focusing attention on the spirit world.

Runes Letters used in the earliest Germanic and Nordic alphabet. Initially a form of writing, the meanings of many of the runes have a quasi-magical significance.

Samsara Sanskrit word meaning 'journeying'. Refers to the endless cycle of existence from one rebirth to the next.

Sidpa The bardo of rebirth.

Soul The thinking, feeling part of a person. The soul is said to live on after the body has died. The 'life force'. St. Augustine, one of Western Christianity's most influential early thinkers, described the soul as a special substance, endowed with reason and adapted to rule the body.

Spirit Inseparable from the soul, the intelligent, immaterial and immortal part of man.

Spirit of Place The special relationship between man and the land.

Spirit releasement Also known as exorcism, a means of releasing spirits found in places, objects or people.

Spirituality Revolution A defining term for the rapid growth of interest in personal spiritual experience in the Western world. A search for meaning.

Torah The five books of the Bible (Genesis, Exodus, Leviticus, Numbers and Deuteronomy).

Tumo Special energy that moves along the chakras enabling the manifestation of deeper spirituality at the point of death.

Universal laws The rules that govern the creation of energy throughout the universe.

Upanishads Ancient Sanskrit religious texts.

White Light Guardians Also known as the 'Occult Police', these are the spiritual guardians of the universe whose mission is to combat the forces of darkness.

White Magic Magic that is used for positive purposes to protect and to heal. The opposite of black magic.

Zohar The primary written work of the Kabbalah (Jewsih mysticism).